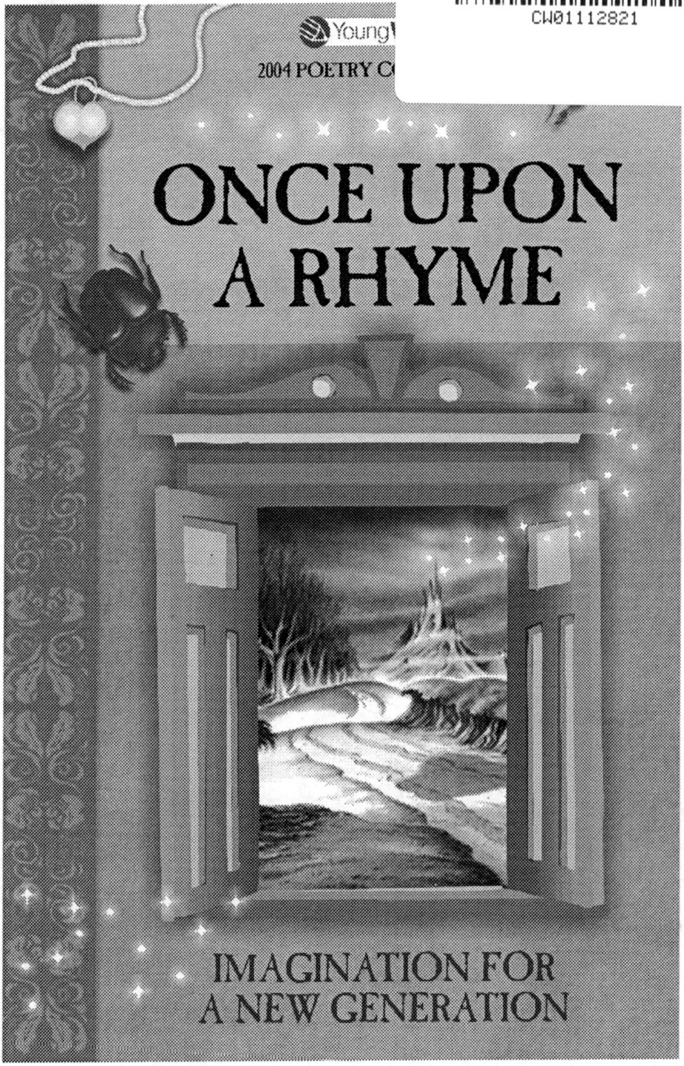
2004 POETRY C
ONCE UPON A RHYME
IMAGINATION FOR A NEW GENERATION

Eastern Counties

Edited by Steve Twelvetree

First published in Great Britain in 2004 by:
Young Writers
Remus House
Coltsfoot Drive
Peterborough
PE2 9JX
Telephone: 01733 890066
Website: www.youngwriters.co.uk

All Rights Reserved

© Copyright Contributors 2004

SB ISBN 1 84460 424 1

Foreword

Young Writers was established in 1991 and has been passionately devoted to the promotion of reading and writing in children and young adults ever since. The quest continues today. Young Writers remains as committed to engendering the fostering of burgeoning poetic and literary talent as ever.

This year's Young Writers competition has proven as vibrant and dynamic as ever and we are delighted to present a showcase of the best poetry from across the UK. Each poem has been carefully selected from a wealth of *Once Upon A Rhyme* entries before ultimately being published in this, our twelfth primary school poetry series.

Once again, we have been supremely impressed by the overall high quality of the entries we have received. The imagination, energy and creativity which has gone into each young writer's entry made choosing the best poems a challenging and often difficult but ultimately hugely rewarding task - the general high standard of the work submitted amply vindicating this opportunity to bring their poetry to a larger appreciative audience.

We sincerely hope you are pleased with our final selection and that you will enjoy *Once Upon A Rhyme Eastern Counties* for many years to come.

Contents

Natasha Leavy (9)   1

Baynards CP School, Colchester
Jessica Gosling (10)   1

Beehive Preparatory School, Ilford
Kajal Kandeth (9)   2
Gajaen Selvarajan (9)   2
Aron Nijjar (9)   3
Charles Obiri Yeboah (8)   3
Zayyaan Zafar (8)   4
Olivia Galvin-Hughes (9)   4
Simran Kaur Chaggar (7)   5
Jordan Day (9)   5

Braeside School, Buckhurst Hill
Georgia Harris-Burdis (11)   6
Nicole Abbott (11)   7
Gabrielle Compton (11)   7
Helen Walker (10)   8

Colney Heath JMI School, St Albans
Sofie Walker (11)   8
Helen Brooks (11)   9
Laura-Jane Dickinson (10)   10
Tommy Cannon (11)   11
Shannon Welch-Mcdonald (10)   12
Gareth Stevenson (10)   12
Thomas Pile (11)   13
Sarah Barnard (10)   14
Rebekah Vennard (10)   15
Oliver Pröslmeyr (10)   16
Hayleigh Clayton (10)   17
Rosie Southward (10)   18
Holly Butler (11)   18
Fiona Wells (10)   19
Sarah Stanley (10)   20

Jessica Everall (10)	21
Nicholas Foster (11)	22
Rebbeka Fox (11)	23

Edwards Hall Junior School, Leigh-on-Sea
Charlotte Goff (9)	24
Jodie Tillson (8)	24
Sam Batchelor (9)	25
Kai Ginn Man (8)	25
Zoe McReynolds (9)	26
Lauren Conway (9)	26
Michaela Convey (9)	27
Nicholas Worrall (8)	27

Holbrook Primary School, Ipswich
Archie Hall (8)	28
Abigail Horne (8)	28
Amy Ravenhall (9)	29
Jack Rennison (9)	30
Jessica Counsell (8)	31
Kieran Harvey (8)	31
Gemma Campbell-Gray (9)	32
Nadine Williams (9)	32
Rachel Garlick (8)	33
Ellë Laming (8)	33
Georgie Harmer (9)	34
Carys Todd (8)	34
Laura Wilding (8)	35
Emily Sweeney (9)	35
Brontë Nicoll (8)	36
Keziah Green (8)	37
Lucy Hall (8)	38

Kenilworth Primary School, Borehamwood
Cherise Ramsey (11)	38
Namwinga Pakhati (11)	39
Carly Agnew (11)	39
Paige Kenny (10)	40
James Gething (11)	40
Amber-Rose Crossley (11)	41

Ellie Kenny (9)	41
Stephanie Toull (11)	42
Shaunnie-Paige Borrett (11)	42
Jack Crawford (11)	43
Chloe Tomkins (11)	43
Billy-Joe Beechey (11)	44
Tanaka Beale (11)	44
Roseanne Chenery (11)	45
Samantha Judd (10)	45
Daryl Joe Lambert (10)	46
Sarah Toull (11)	46
Daniella Villiers (10)	47
Lee Michael Woodhouse (11)	47
Jodie Reilly (8)	48
Rianna Moule (11)	48
Karl Bourne (11)	49
Molly McDonagh (9)	49
Oliver Bassil (8)	50
Tala Sweiss (9)	50
Leanne Murray (8)	51
Danielle Wesley (8)	51
Hollie Coombes (9)	52
Eleanor Marshall (9)	53
Lee Antony Lindsay (11)	54

Little Gaddesden Primary School, Berkhamsted

Katie Vest (10)	54
Katherine Cannon (9)	55
Kate Rogers (11)	56
Thomas Gaden Nicholson	57
Harry Jeffersen-Perry (10)	58
Jennifer Cannon (11)	59
Stephen Berry (10)	60
Jack Elkes (10)	61
Laura Barthorpe (11)	62
Eleanor Humphreys (10)	63
Georgia McCarthy (10)	63
Sarah Hocking (10)	64
Rebekah Holden (10)	65
Heather Musgrave (10)	66

Maldon Court Prep School, Maldon
Jack English (11)	66
Christopher Millidge (10)	67
Callum Bugler (11)	67
Cordelia Cumbers (10)	67
Joshua Carter (11)	68
James Baron (10)	68
Rosie Coppin (11)	69
Alice Walder (11)	69
Oliver Heward (10)	69
Courtney Granger (11)	70
Jessica Quinlan (10)	70
Stephanie Baron (11)	71

Maltman's Green School, Gerrards Cross
Madeline Seifert (10)	72
Georgia Hanscott (10)	72
Emily Gravestock (10)	73
Leticia Baxter (11)	73
Gemma North (11)	74
Lara Shepherd (11)	74
Ayisha Gulati (10)	75
Kim Phillips-Page (10)	75
Katrina Baxter (11)	76
Hannah Dorkin (11)	76
Natasha Williams (9)	77
Grace Joseph (10)	77
Amarantha Wells (10)	77
Alicia Ptaszynska-Neophytou (11)	78
Gemma Samworth (11)	78
Zoë Chambers (10)	79
Charlotte Gilham (10)	79
Shivani Patel (10)	79
Gabriella Long (9)	80
Clare Newell (10)	80
Emily Eastwood (9)	80
Amabel Clark (10)	81
Alexandra Wiseman (10)	81
Victoria Foden (10)	81
Emma Louise Goodey (11)	82
Marie-Sophie Daniels (11)	82

Rebecca Dev (10)	83
Lucy Tibble (9)	83
Shabri Chandarana (9)	83
Samantha Foskett (10)	84
Christina Osborne (11)	84
Hayley Garnham (10)	84
Lydia Crawley (10)	85
Charlotte Child (11)	85
Betty Makharinsky (10)	85
Hannah Beattie (10)	86
Zoë Kearley (10)	86
Emily Baines (10)	86

Mundford CE VC Primary School, Thetford

Toni Campbell (10)	87
Natalie Cosstick (10)	88
Elouise Marenghi (11)	88
Alexandra Summers (11)	89
Scott Palmer (11)	89
Michael Brown (11)	90
Merrick Haglund (10)	90
Alice Dolton (9)	91
Georgia Morris (10)	91
Kirsty Campbell Hibbs (10)	92
Betsie Nelson (10)	93
Cody Pumper (11)	94
Paige Gooch (10)	94
Sam Rodé (10)	94
Benjamin Clark (10)	95

Myland Primary School, Colchester

Blake Benjamin (11)	95
Aimée Jade Artus (11)	96
Lauren Humbles (11)	96
Robert Beauchamp (11)	97
Karl Lloyd (11)	97
Heather Wald (11)	98
Liam Eaton (11) & Keith Ajagun-Brauns (10)	98
Niall Rudd (11)	99
Alice Bryant (11)	99
Lelan Spence (8)	99

Karthik Chandrasekharan (10)	100
James Buckley (11)	101
Bethany Pike (11)	101
Izzy Sagnella (10)	102
Jessica Saunders (8)	102
Natascha Lopez (10)	102
Jade Basshier (11)	103
Helen Burt (11)	103
Lewis Baker (7)	104
Sabastian Lever (7)	104
Jade Chenery (11)	104
Michelle Li (10)	105
Hari Kaarthik Chokkalingam (8)	105
Georgia Tokely (8)	106
Christopher Cooper (8)	106
Jordan Graham (8)	106
Rhea Gopaul (8)	107
Gemma Willett (8)	107
Lauren Mott (7)	107

Old Heath Primary School, Colchester
Shaun Duplock	108
Emily Evans (6)	109

Priory School, Southend-on-Sea
Luke Murphy (9)	109

Roundwood Primary School, Harpenden
Joe Graham (11)	110
Sophie Frost (10)	110
Lucy Randall (10)	111
Daniella Allard (10)	111
Timothy Chisnall (11)	112
Rebecca Cave (11)	112
Dan Wells (10)	113
Thomas Kearns (10)	113
Sarah Hodge (11)	114
Tara Cornes (10)	114
Theodore Green (10)	115
Rory Williams (10)	115
Olivia O'Neill (10)	116

Charlotte Scott (10)	117
Rory Scott (11)	118
Matthew Corcoran (10)	119
James Gray (10)	120
Bob Palmer (10)	121
Lucinda Scholey (11)	122
Dominic Childs (11)	122
Greg Nelson (11)	123
Christopher Featherstone (11)	123
Dylan Hopkins (11)	124
Samuel Rose (11)	124

St Aubyns Preparatory School, Woodford Green

James Crosby (11)	125
Maria Ruffy (11)	125
Ammen Gill (11)	126
Amelia Ruff (10)	126
Freddie Sayer (10)	127
Jonathan Lalude (10)	127
Aditya Banerjee (11)	128
Matthew Michell (10)	129
Leon Haxby (10)	129
Raymond Parkinson (10)	130
Peter Joseph (11)	131
Jennifer Shaw (10)	132
Sameer Farooq (10)	133
Mehmet-Can Akkaya (11)	134
Binta Balogun (10)	134
Aruna Pahwa (10)	135
Mario Mastantuono ((9)	135
Ross Partridge (11)	136
George Kingsley (7)	136
Harry Ellis-Grewal (10)	137
Maisha Ali (8)	137
Christian Pannell (11)	138
Emma Myers (10)	139
Bethany Lamb (8)	140
Gabriella Bloom (8)	140
George Bayles (9)	141
Georgina Colton (9)	141
Aisha Hussain (8)	142

Sophie Roberts (9)	142
Harjay Singh Sehmi (9)	143
Bomi Babalola (9)	143
Haseeb Yusuf (9)	144
Edward R Graves (10)	144
Joseph Baum (10)	145
Gabriel Keegan (10)	145
Aaqib Anwar (11)	146
Rachel Mortlock (7)	147
Nicholas Dixon (11)	147
James Carter (9)	148
Thomas Hartington (10)	149
Alexander Tudor (8)	149
Adara Wicaksono (9)	150
Isabel Roberts (8)	150
Sophie Bishop (8)	151
Sam Bromley (8)	151
Ben Wernick (9)	152
Crichelle Brice (8)	153
Rhianne Saunders (9)	154
Jack Drew (10)	155
Nicole Barbour (9)	156

St Helen's Primary School, Ipswich

Owen Rees (8)	156
Christopher Boyt (10)	157
Hannah Erin Turner (8)	157
Hannah Barron (9)	158
Hannah Pugh (9)	158
Jethro Franklin (10)	159
Louise Lear (10)	159
Sean Johnson (9)	160
Emily Barron (11)	160
Jade Cavanagh (10)	161
Eleanor Turner (9)	161
Hal Rudkin (10)	162
George Tobin (10)	162
Amber E Durrant (10)	163
Henrik Anderson (9)	163
Lauren Flood (10)	164
Jacob Sharlott Sewell (9)	164

Rukshana Aktar (10)	165
Mhari Grant (10)	165
Elaine Rees (11)	166
Georgina Anstee (9)	166
Emma Williams (9)	167
Hannah Cotton (9)	167
Sangeeta Kaur (10)	168
Chloe Etherington (9)	168
Harry Smithson (10)	169
Marcus Kuzvinzwa (10)	169
William Johnson (9)	170
Amy Forrester (9)	170
Rebecca Moore (11)	171
Rujina Begum (10)	171
Emily Richards (10)	172
Stephen Caliguiri (9)	172
Maisie Clarke (8)	173
Hudson G Shoults (9)	173
Lily Buckley (11)	174

St Luke's RC Primary School, Harlow

Tamsin Hurton (10)	174
Karen O'Callaghan (10)	175
Carla Mortimer (10)	175
Jessica Beere (10)	176
Chad England (10)	176
Jack Doyle (11)	177
Rakeem Dixon (10)	177
Tom Juliff (10)	178
Emma Rogers (10)	178
Annie Groome (10)	179
Jennifer O'Keeffe (11)	179
Kelly Lynch (10)	180
Amy Jade Stean (10)	180
Claire Pearman (10)	181
Natalie Bell (10)	181
Shannon Molloy (10)	182
Dalton Chamberlain (11)	182
Georgia Souter (9)	183
Louise Spiller (11)	183
Eddie Njenga (10)	184

Maria Lynch (11)	184
Nicole Ray (10)	185
Ryan Melaugh (9)	185
Jamie Dawson (10)	185
Sarah Humphreys (10)	186
Shannon Eley (11)	186
Louisa Findell (10)	187
Jordan Allen (9)	187
Mitchell Seymour (9)	188
Kirsty Hitchen (9)	188
Hayley Hughes (9)	189
Robert Millwaters (9)	189
Ryan Matthew (10)	189
Teresa Holdstock (10)	190
Megan Stent (9)	190
Eigdmear McCrudden (9)	190
Lauren Luque (8)	191
Amy Bassett (8)	191
Rhianna Coulson (8)	191
Khadijah Green (9)	192
Helena Peppiatt (8)	192
Mollie Thomas (8)	192
Daniel Lloyd (9)	193
Daniella Parr (9)	193
Charlie Kiernan (9)	193
Peitro Randazzo (11)	194
Daniel Munden (9)	194
Matthew Addicott (8)	194
Daniel Jackson (8)	195
Nicola Beere (8)	195
Conor Molloy (9)	195
Ruth Nulty (8)	196
Matthew Browne (9)	196

The Bishops' CE & RC Primary School, Chelmsford

Michael Jeffery (10)	196
Lucy Kirkby (10)	197
Lauren Gillingham (10)	197
Emily Nicholls (10)	198
Thomas Storkey (10)	198
Nathanael Rogers (10)	199

Steven Thompson-Friend (10)	199
Thomas Went (9)	200
Lucinda Andrews (9)	200
Stuart Belbin (10)	201
Katie Brown (9)	201
Roisin Chapman (9)	202
Alex Collop (10)	202
Adam Cresswell (10)	203
Lianne Shepherd (9)	203
Claire Parker (9)	204
Stephanie Thompson (10)	204
Heidi Smith (9)	205
Laura Edes (10)	205
Ben Seago (10)	206
Keifer Teahan (9)	206
Lucy McDonald (9)	206
Jamie Haines (9)	207
Conor Stephens (10)	207
Danielle Bailey (10)	208
Emily Siddaway (9)	209
George Cove (9)	209
Jade Gibson (9)	210
Caitlin Edwards (9)	210
Megan Evans (9)	210
Rachel Myers (9)	211
Naomi French (9)	211

William Read Primary School, Canvey Island

Ryan Thorn (8)	212
Elise Radley (8)	212
Edward Pettitt (8)	212
Jay Lynch (9)	213
Lacey Amanda Young (8)	213
Chloe Gower (8)	213
Meltem Sahan (9)	214
Clarice Witt (9)	214
Desma Tucker (9)	215
Ashleigh Dawson (8)	215
Brooke Pidgeon (9)	216
Jack Sanders (9)	216
Amber Cole (8)	217

Daniela Livornese (8)	217
Jack Myles (8)	217
Jessica Denney (8)	218
Elliott Bracci (9)	218
Alice Ison (8)	218
Brooke Osborn (8)	219
Caryna Barr (8)	219
Zara Preston (8)	220
Natasha Kelkar (8)	220
Sam Waters (8)	220
Harrison Mockett (8)	221
Harley Skidmore (9)	221
Adam Sartain (9)	222
Joe Denham (8)	222
Jordan Blackwell (9)	223
Scott Stone (9)	223

The Poems

My Big Baboon

My big baboon is shaped like a balloon
He has a big head and loves my Uncle Ted
When we go to stay with him he squeezes him
All day and all night
He is a big laugh, he's my big baboon
That's all for now about my big baboon
Bye-bye, hope to see you soon.

Natasha Leavy (9)

Please Don't Do It

Please stay calm,
You don't need to take it,
It will be such a shame,
It will ruin everything.

There's a battle in your head,
Please don't take it,
It won't solve your problems,
It will ruin everything.

There, sitting in a church,
All dressed in black,
Crying and sobbing,
You've ruined everything.

We told you not to do it.

Jessica Gosling (10)
Baynards CP School, Colchester

A Very, Very, Very Wacky Musketeer

There was once a musketeer
Whose name was Christopher Calear
Who was a wacky one
And couldn't get the job done.
So once a day
He would watch a weird play
Trying to find a lesson
Yet failed every wacky session.
If he got angry and yelled
He would surely get pelled
And the children said he smelled!
He didn't care
Of what he did wear
For usually it did tear.
He would cry
If he got hit by a fly.
There was once a musketeer
Who had a queer name
And there is no other who is the same!

Kajal Kandeth (9)
Beehive Preparatory School, Ilford

Winter

Cold as ice as frozen ponds
as slippery as gold

As leaves fall down
when ducks freeze to death

And girls and boys
skate with joy

It's fun to play when
everybody plays with snow

But the only thing is
dads and mums don't let us play.

Gajaen Selvarajan (9)
Beehive Preparatory School, Ilford

My Dog Jay

My dog Jay is very happy,
But he doesn't need to wear a nappy.
He lies on the floor in the morning,
But sun leaves in the afternoon.
Me and my dog Jay wear shades,
I take him out for a walk,
But someday I wish I could talk.
He's good at football and baseball,
But he's excellent at basketball.
My dog Jay is like my best friend,
He's so cool, he's had an award from George W Bush.
He's such a good American dog.
He's had four black eyes,
But now he's got a black eye that will stay forever.
I love my dog Jay.

Aron Nijjar (9)
Beehive Preparatory School, Ilford

Mike And Fog

There was once a boy called Mike
He liked wearing Nike.

Mike hated school
Like most kids do.

It started when he had something in his shoe
Mike had a dog called Fog because he sat on a log.

After his dog died
Mike never lied.

When his friends heard the news
They all burst out with 'phews'.

But when Mike asked, 'Is my dog in trouble?'
The friends said, 'No,
But he gets us in a double.'

Charles Obiri Yeboah (8)
Beehive Preparatory School, Ilford

The Confusing Poem

I did it right
but my needle fell out of sight
and I hope it didn't poke in the bright
and then I saw it sitting in fright
but it jumped again
and I was insane
when it was the afternoon
I still couldn't see it soon
and I saw it bloom
and it flew away
and I never saw it again
but it came back
and said
' Why are you lurking about?'
I got angry
and I caught it
and put it in the needle box tin.

Zayyaan Zafar (8)
Beehive Preparatory School, Ilford

Weather

I see the sun shining on the grassy hills.
I see the snow falling upon the treetops.
I see the raindrops glisten on the window sill.
I see the clouds darken in the misty sky.
I see the stars twinkling in the night air.
I see the moon glowing in a most beautiful way.

This all leads up to thinking about weather
Which is part of what created Earth.
And now we enjoy all weathers because
Otherwise we wouldn't be here on Earth today.

Olivia Galvin-Hughes (9)
Beehive Preparatory School, Ilford

Summer

It was a sunny day
So I went out to play
I played till late at night
My mum came and gave me a fright
She said I had to go to bed
I went to bed till the next day
So I could go and play
I woke up at three o'clock
I put my clothes on and on went my socks
I looked at the time
It was three o'clock
And the clock hadn't even chimed
I went back to sleep
And the alarm clock went *beep beep beep*
To play with the sun
Hooray.

Simran Kaur Chaggar (7)
Beehive Preparatory School, Ilford

Shiny, Bright, Big Star

Shiny, bright, big star
How you wander out so far

Shiny, bright, big star
How you hover through the night

Shiny, bright, big star
You're as bright as a night light

Shiny, bright, big star
What do you like o'er the moon or
Round the world?

Shiny, bright, big star
You say goodbye and enter the bright.

Jordan Day (9)
Beehive Preparatory School, Ilford

The Monster's Romance

There once was a monster, who lived in a cave
The problem was he didn't know how to behave
He never had a wash or changed his clothes
So everybody walked with a peg on their nose
His table manners were oh so bad
This made his mother very, very sad
One day in the village a maiden he saw
Who made him stop and stand in awe
He went to his mother to ask for a makeover
In order to win the fair maiden's heart over
His mother screamed then had a good laugh
Took him by the ear and gave him a bath
She washed his clothes and cut his hair
He was then ready to win the maiden fair
Flowers and chocolates he went and bought
Then to the village, the maiden to court
He strutted down the village, smart and clean
This was a sight they had never seen
He and the maiden went to the park
And chatted and chatted until it grew dark
Off to the shop to buy a ring
And at the church the whole village did sing
This is the end of the story, we're told
And now they are a sight to behold
Now clean and smart wherever they go
And no peg on a villager ever to show.

Georgia Harris-Burdis (11)
Braeside School, Buckhurst Hill

Behind The Door

'Behind the door, on the first floor
. . . is the Iron Man who's ever so ugly, though,'
said my big bro.

'Behind the door, on the first floor
. . . is a beautiful princess who needs to be awakened
by true love's kiss,' said my big sis.

'Behind the door, on the first floor
. . . is the Pied Piper, who's a jolly old lad,' said my dad.

'Behind the door, on the first floor
. . . is a dragon who eats little boys,
so you'd better run,' said my mum.

'Behind the door, on the first floor
. . . is a fiendish ghost,' said the man who brings the post.

But I know they're only kiddin'
behind the door is Mum's bed linen.

Nicole Abbott (11)
Braeside School, Buckhurst Hill

When I Grow Up

When I grow up I want to be a famous face,
go into space
or even win an Olympic race.

When I grow up I want to be a vet
fly a jet
or even buy some houses to let.

When I grow up I want to be a . . .
policeman!

Gabrielle Compton (11)
Braeside School, Buckhurst Hill

Autumn

Crunching leaves under my feet
Trees swaying in the wind above me
Autumn is here.
Warm indoors, cold outside
Leaves changing colour
Brown, red, yellow and gold
Glinting cobwebs in the morning light
Sleepy spiders from their night hunt
In the forest that's where I like to go.

Quiet and lonely, under the shady trees,
In the dense undergrowth I love to wonder
Squirrels collecting acorns and beechnuts
Foxes patrolling their territories
Hedgehogs ready for hibernation, burrowing under the leaves
Robins with their bright red breasts chirp amongst the trees.

Nature is alive but resting.

Helen Walker (10)
Braeside School, Buckhurst Hill

Once Upon A Rhyme

All the boys outside playing a game,
All the girls practising for fame.

All the girls standing slim and tall,
All the boys acting the fool.

All the boys do nothing but play,
All the girls making the most of their day.

All the girls sitting nice in their chair,
All the boys wishing they weren't there.

All the boys putting up a fight,
All the girls being kind and polite.

Sofie Walker (11)
Colney Heath JMI School, St Albans

Once Upon A Rhyme

Stars that sparkle in the night,
they are such a beautiful sight.

Twinkle, twinkle little star,
as I watch them from the car.

Above the clouds so high,
before I sleep I say goodbye.

What makes them shine and gleam?
They make a winning team.

Are they pointed, are they round -
can the answers ever be found?

We watch them from near and far,
what are you, little mystery star?

When the day is done,
they appear to replace the sun.

What's their value, I wonder as I stare,
would they make us a millionaire?

Am I the only one that cares,
or are there other people that watch and stare?

On a background so deep and dark
as if a firework with a spark.

I know I'm asking lots of questions,
but they are such good suggestions.

If it is a cloudy night,
they can't possibly shine so bright.

Masked by fluffy black and grey
they seem to push the clouds away.

Stars shining bright, please don't go,
you are such a wonderful show.

You've disappeared in the morning,
even though I'm still yawning.

Helen Brooks (11)
Colney Heath JMI School, St Albans

Once Upon A Rhyme

On the edge of a deep, dark wood
there lived a little girl called
Little Red Riding Hood

Her grandmother lived not far away,
so Little Red Riding Hood
went to see her one day

But there was a big bad wolf
who knew her plan
he stood up and ran and ran

He came to a stop at her grandmother's door
then he ate her up with a great loud roar

He crept into her nice warm bed and
waited there for Little Miss Red
then there was a knock at the door -

In she came to see her gran
she looked in the bed and she said, 'Hello!'
then realised it was a wolf instead

She screamed and ran down the path
bumped into the woodcutter who cut
the wolf in half.
Then Gran got out safely!

Laura-Jane Dickinson (10)
Colney Heath JMI School, St Albans

Once Upon A Rhyme

Don't go away
And do not stray
I will tell you a story
Which makes me jump in glory

With my friends just walking
And we were all talking
I heard a cry for help
And minutes later heard a yelp

There was no light
The noise gave me a fright
My friends dashed off
Into the night

I looked around
And there I found
A very old woman on the ground

She said that she had been attacked
And her handbag had been ransacked.

I helped her up and called my dad
Who said that it was really sad
That old people are easy prey
Especially in our world today.

Tommy Cannon (11)
Colney Heath JMI School, St Albans

Once Upon A Rhyme

There was a cat called Bob
who liked the fish cod
Bob went for a stroll
and saw a little foal
he saw a boy eating fish
so he started to wish
he heard a song
it went on for so long
he fell asleep
on someone's feet
Bob woke up with a fright
oh no! It was nearly night
Bob jumped over gates
and near some lakes
he had a break
oh dear, it was too late
the lights were off
so Bob couldn't sleep on anything soft
he scratched his head
because his owners went to bed.

Shannon Welch-Mcdonald (10)
Colney Heath JMI School, St Albans

Once Upon A Rhyme

Once upon a rhyme
There was an ancient porcupine,
It lived in a tower up in the air,
He knew a girl with very long hair.

The girl sang to him every day,
But she didn't sing to him yesterday.
The porcupine was really unhappy,
And he became very snappy.

The girl came back from jail
And the porcupine never knew the tale.

Gareth Stevenson (10)
Colney Heath JMI School, St Albans

Once Upon A Rhyme

There once was a time
When all must rhyme,
From the ocean floor
To the land's front door.

But then one day
A bird called Jay,
Had had enough
Of rhyming stuff.

'This is absurd!'
Cried out the bird.
'Why must we rhyme
And waste our time?'

So on that day
He flew away,
To see the chief
Of the rhyming reef.

'Excuse me Sir,'
Said the bird from Chir,
'It can't be a crime,
If we don't always rhyme.'

The chief told a tale
Of an angry whale,
Who would stop all time
If we didn't rhyme.

'And so you see
Little birdie,
We have to rhyme,
To keep our time.'

Thomas Pile (11)
Colney Heath JMI School, St Albans

Once Upon A Rhyme

Cinderella was about to put on her dress
When she realised that the castle was still a big mess

So she went back and scrubbed the floors
And then after that, she polished the doors

Cinderella then put on her beautiful frock
When at the door there came a knock

It was her fairy godmother, standing still and proud
Then her stepsisters entered and screamed very loud

As she put on her shoes and said, 'What's the matter?'
They all looked at each other and started to natter

Cinderella said to them, 'Why are you staring at me?'
And as she said it, she got stung by a bee

Cinderella went to the nurse, who said, 'Let me see!'
She lifted her frock and there was her swollen knee

When she got home she thought it was half-past seven
But when she looked at the clock, it was actually eleven

So she put her pyjamas on and got into bed
And in the morning she woke up with a bit of a sore head

Luckily, after her breakfast she felt much better
And then through the post came a letter

Cinderella opened it and read it out very clear
With her stepsisters extremely near

The prince declared his love so true
And said, I want to marry you.

Sarah Barnard (10)
Colney Heath JMI School, St Albans

Once Upon A Rhyme

Once upon a rhyme
In a faraway land
There was a beautiful beach
With fine golden sand.

Upon this beach
Under a stone
Was a little beach creature
His name was Jerome.

This strange little creature
Was a funny old thing
It had eighteen legs
And a tail that would sting.

Now Jerome, he liked
To travel around
Looking for shellfish
Under the ground.

Jerome met a crab
And a lobster one day
They soon became friends
And they all liked to play.

Now having a friend
Is a wonderful thing
But you have to be careful
If one's got a sting.

When playing around
By the sea on a rock
Jerome's mighty tail
Gave poor lobster a shock.

Jerome's friends have now gone away
And Jerome feels lonely with no one to play.

Rebekah Vennard (10)
Colney Heath JMI School, St Albans

Once Upon A Rhyme

Once upon a time
A little black cat
Was born under a shed
Well fancy that!

The litter of kittens were born
Underneath the shed
Sadly she lived
The others were dead

The mother cat reacted
In a very sad way
The little black cat
Was now a stray

She spent the first few months
Alone in the barn
With only mice for company
And out of any harm

Then one lucky day
A boy came by
'I'd love to take you home
And have you by my side

I'll call you Sarah
My lucky, black cat
I'll give you lots of love
And never shout back.'

Sarah went home
With Oliver (me) that day
And ever since that time
Has the whole day to play

Once upon a time
Stories can come true
Listen to Sarah's story
Next time, it might be lucky you.

Oliver Pröslmeyr (10)
Colney Heath JMI School, St Albans

Once Upon A Rhyme

Once upon a rhyme,
A long, long time ago,
Where golden unicorns did fly,
And foals were born in snow.

Once upon a rhyme,
Where there was a thrilling breeze,
A little bunny hopped along
Straight past the blossom trees.

Once upon a rhyme,
Disaster was in the air,
The trees were rocking and everyone was relaying
Beware, beware, *beware!*

Once upon a rhyme,
Came a disastrous young man,
Who cut down trees and ran through breeze,
And killed every single lamb.

Once upon a rhyme,
To everyone a letter was sent,
Calling a meeting that night for the action plan,
That night the rules of peace were bent.

Once upon a rhyme
The young man was cutting down more trees,
When out jumped the bunny with a sword in his paw
And with the man's head he hopped back calmly through the breeze.

Once upon a rhyme
A long time ago,
Where golden unicorns did fly
And foals were born in snow.

Hayleigh Clayton (10)
Colney Heath JMI School, St Albans

Once Upon A Rhyme

Once upon a rhyme,
Long, long ago.
There was a beautiful wonderland,
Covered in glistening snow.

Rivers twining and skies so blue,
Colourful fishes racing the waves.
The whitest sands you could ever imagine,
Fires burning in deep, dark caves.

Unicorns galloping across the plains,
The sounds of birds singing at dawn.
The smell of hope is floating about
In spring, summer, autumn, winter the prettiest flowers are born.

The tallest trees, cherry blossom,
Squirrels hiding in nature's hands,
The loveliest views from high and low,
That's my beautiful wonderland.

Rosie Southward (10)
Colney Heath JMI School, St Albans

What Is In My Bedroom

In my room is a box
In my room is a writing desk
In my room is a toy ox
That is what is in my room

In my room is a TV
In my room is a teddy bear
In my room is a photo of me
That is what is in my room

In my room is a big bed
In my room is a computer
In my room, it is red
That is what is in my room.

Holly Butler (11)
Colney Heath JMI School, St Albans

Once Upon A Rhyme

When I was just a bonnie lass
My father told me so,
That there was a stunning dolphin,
As white as purest snow.

So I searched for the dolphin,
Through sea after sea,
Till there came a time,
It never could be.

Then upon my boat,
Came a bright, luminous shine.
The dolphin leapt up and chuckled with joy,
A beautiful, enchanting rhyme.

'Oh what is your name?' I sang merrily,
'You need not know!' he clicked and he chuckled
Then all of a sudden he vanished beneath,
Splashing me with waves, so cold my knees buckled.

Now why should I tell this story as a poem?
With no great white sharks or green mouldy slime.
Because his name is so simply perfect -
It's
Once Upon A Rhyme.

Fiona Wells (10)
Colney Heath JMI School, St Albans

Once Upon A Rhyme

Loraine, oh Loraine
As you walk down the lane
The flowers all covered
With droplets of rain.

Loraine, oh Loraine,
To the school gate you came
The headmaster's waiting,
Saying, 'You're late again!'

Loraine, oh Loraine
To the classroom you came
The lesson was disrupted
But girl you'll get the cane!

Walking back home
It has started to rain,
'Oh what a pain,'
Says little Loraine.

Her mother is waiting
With a smile on her face
'Hurry Loraine,
Stop staring into space!'

Sarah Stanley (10)
Colney Heath JMI School, St Albans

Once Upon A Rhyme

Once upon a rhyme in a beautiful land
Lived horses of many colours,
Apart from one who was very grand,
Who didn't mix with the others.

This creature was a unicorn,
Had fur of dazzling white,
Upon his head a golden horn,
Which sparkled as he galloped.

This unicorn had magic powers,
Which came from its golden horn,
Weeds and nettles turned into flowers,
Whenever he galloped past.

Many tried to catch this magical creature,
Using tricks of many kinds,
To use his horn as a feature,
But all have miserably failed.

This creature, he was very kind,
He wanted to help all,
Everyone happiness to find,
Once upon a rhyme!

Jessica Everall (10)
Colney Heath JMI School, St Albans

Once Upon A Rhyme

Once upon a rhyme
There were fairies and pixies
That all day long granted wishes and flew

Once upon a rhyme
There were goblins and gremlins
That terrorised the fairies and ate all the pixies

Once upon a rhyme
There were leprechauns from Ireland
Who left you a pot of gold at the end of the rainbow

Once upon a rhyme
There were unicorns in the forest
That hid in the moonlight and lived in the woods

Once upon a rhyme
There were elves in the sky
That roamed on the clouds of winter nights

Once upon a rhyme
There were mystical creatures
That lived on the earth and hid from the humans.

Nicholas Foster (11)
Colney Heath JMI School, St Albans

Once Upon A Rhyme

Once upon a rhyme,

Tweedle Dum and Tweedle Dee
Came round for some tea
They ate all the pie
I thought they might die

Tweedle Dum and Tweedle Dee
Left nothing for me
All they did was sleep and snooze
They just woke up for the ten o'clock news

Tweedle Dum and Tweedle Dee
Had both got fleas
I will never have them again
I thought about sending them home on the train

Tweedle Dum and Tweedle Dee they told me
They'd lost their key
So they decided they had to stay
I wished I could fade away!

Rebbeka Fox (11)
Colney Heath JMI School, St Albans

Rain

Spitting down, so careful not to harm
it's a falling lullaby singing sweetly,
watery eyes like a child about to cry
silver drops which look like diamonds falling.

Suddenly it hammers down,
flooding the Earth,
teeming, making us run away,
flooding the Earth like a big angry monster
making the gutters overflow.

The rain calms down
and starts to spit again,
children happy to play,
peace has arrived.

Charlotte Goff (9)
Edwards Hall Junior School, Leigh-on-Sea

Rain

Slowly the tiny angel's tears trickle down
the golden drops like a lullaby,
the drops bounce off the window.

The rain gets fierce, smacking you
it's like cupid shooting his arrows down to Earth.

The rain is a baby crying
slowly it calms down
and the sun comes out.

Jodie Tillson (8)
Edwards Hall Junior School, Leigh-On-Sea

Rain

The rain pit-pats on your face
Tip-tapping on the roof,
It's like an army of shimmering swords spitting down,
It's a ballerina dancing on the windowpane.

The rain suddenly turns into a hideous storm
Like all the gods striking the land with angry spears,
It gets angrier by the second.

Then rain calms down
and brings peace again.
Little children come out again
as happy as happy dreams.

Sam Batchelor (9)
Edwards Hall Junior School, Leigh-On-Sea

Rain

The glittering rain
Flows like a kite flying in the sky
Splashing on the road making people soaked.

It is as cold as snow
It is as beautiful as the sunshine.

The rain is dropping from the grey cloud
Like bombs falling from a jet in the sky,
It is splashing and roaring down the gutter,
The rain is banging and smashing the ground as hard as it can.

Kai Ginn Man (8)
Edwards Hall Junior School, Leigh-On-Sea

The River

The river's water is calm and peaceful,
Running over the pebbles,
That shine in the gleaming water,
Due to the sun's powerful rays.

The quiet trickling noise,
Fills the salty air,
As calm as a mouse,
Hiding in the grass beside the river bank.

And then it comes to a halt,
Of its journey of nature,
It bursts out its banks into the sea,
Never to be seen again.

Zoe McReynolds (9)
Edwards Hall Junior School, Leigh-On-Sea

The Sea

The calm sea has little ripples,
Massaging the golden sand,
The gentle waves make little breezes,
Running through your hair.

Without warning it becomes anguished,
Like bears arguing and crashing boats.

The stormy sea calms down
As it gets tired and falls asleep.

Lauren Conway (9)
Edwards Hall Junior School, Leigh-On-Sea

The Sea

The gentle sea ripples
Stroking the golden sand,
Creating froth and foam
Like a big bathtub with bubbles.

Without warning it can become deadly
Like a vicious battle with swords and shooting,
From the sea onto the sand.

The raging sea slowly calms down
Producing a peaceful and gentle rhythm,
As smooth as a mother wrapping a blanket around you
The sea draws us in.

Michaela Convey (9)
Edwards Hall Junior School, Leigh-On-Sea

The Sea

The calm sea is composed,
Casting white froth across the sand,
Like a waterfall stroking.

Without warning it can rage
Like a rhinoceros charging,
The sea is stormy,
Crashing and bashing.

Slowly the waves start to lie down
Becoming as flat as a pancake
And as calm as a gentle breeze,
Making it like a swimming pool.

Nicholas Worrall (8)
Edwards Hall Junior School, Leigh-On-Sea

Sometimes

Sometimes I like to cuddle my cat,
To stroke him and stroke him
Till he purrs at me back.

Sometimes I want to sit by the fire,
To watch the coals and the flames
And simply admire.

Sometimes I dream about having a dog,
I've promised to walk him,
Even at 6 o'clock.

Sometimes I need to go on the computer,
My brother won't help me,
But I think he ought to.

Sometimes I ride my small motorbike,
But only in France with my dad . . .
Which I like.

But sometimes I have to sit and do homework,
Write poems, do sums,
Just lots and lots of hard work!

Archie Hall (8)
Holbrook Primary School, Ipswich

Jinks Kenning

Eyes glaring,
Claws scratching,
Tail wagging,
Ears pointing,
Nose sniffing,
Stripes swirling,
My tabby cat.

Abigail Horne (8)
Holbrook Primary School, Ipswich

My Brothers And Sisters

Matthew is the oldest,
We don't always get on,
But he makes up good games
And we all play along.

Hannah is next,
Bossy is she,
She lets me borrow her clothes,
That can also fit me.

Then it's me,
My name is Amy,
They say I'm moody
And really sporty.

Charlotte is next,
The annoying one,
She's my roommate
And we can have fun.

Then it's Emily,
The biggest twin,
She is sweet
With her grin.

Lydia is next,
The cheeky one,
She makes friends
With everyone.

Then comes Daniel,
The youngest of all,
He loves his Sylvester
And has just started school.

Amy Ravenhall (9)
Holbrook Primary School, Ipswich

Some We Win

Cutting through the mud and rain,
A huge crowd buzzing in my brain.
The heavy ball is delivered to my feet,
Expectations I must meet.
Top right hand corner is in my mind,
Oh why is life so unkind?
I have hit the ball way over the bar,
It quickly flew far too far.

The opposition take a goal kick,
Their forwards are lightning quick.
Our lazy defence is caught sleeping,
Their big striker is slowly creeping,
He easily picks up the ball,
Our keeper is a clumsy fool.
The ball rockets into the back of his net,
He has never saved a good shot yet.

1-0 is the latest score,
The crowd let out a mighty roar.
There is only 3 minutes left to go
And my heart is heavy and full of woe.
We cannot afford to lose the game,
My worried team hang their heads in shame.
The final whistle is eventually blown
And now our fate is finally known.

Jack Rennison (9)
Holbrook Primary School, Ipswich

I've Got A Dog Called Bentley

I've got a dog named Bentley
I treat him very gently
I love him very much
He is so soft to touch
We have lots of fun
When we take him for a run
He searches the hedgerows
And sniffs and sniffs
Everywhere he goes
When we get home
He's tired and goes to his bed
Where he rests his
Sleepy head.

Jessica Counsell (8)
Holbrook Primary School, Ipswich

Playing Away

Jumping away,
Running all day,
Hiding from the cops,
I've got to go.

I'll see you tomorrow,
I've got to do some jobs,
I'm running away,
I've done the jumping today.

I stole some hay,
I swung away,
From the cops all day
And saved the day.

Kieran Harvey (8)
Holbrook Primary School, Ipswich

Spocks And Wocks (Space Creatures)

The stars in the sky,
That twinkle your eye,
Hold secrets from us all.

The craters you may think are holes,
Made from falling rocks,
Are actually the homes,
To lots of little spocks.

The spocks have lots
Of little balls,
To bounce and bounce away,
Against the crater walls.

The Wocks are lots of
Tall, tall trees
With lots of branches
And lots and lots of leaves.

So that's all from me and
The little Spocks
The cold, red planet
And the tall, tall Wocks.

Gemma Campbell-Gray (9)
Holbrook Primary School, Ipswich

The Fish Pie

Once I saw a little fish
Swimming into shore,
I caught it with my fishing rod,
It didn't swim no more.

Nadine Williams (9)
Holbrook Primary School, Ipswich

Snow

The air is cold,
The sky is grey,
It looks like snow,
Is coming today.

It's now mid-winter,
Christmas has gone,
The snow has settled
We're all having fun.

A day off school,
We played in the snow,
We built a snowman
And made snowballs to throw.

The night drew in,
There was frost about,
The stars shone brightly
And the moon came out.

Rachel Garlick (8)
Holbrook Primary School, Ipswich

My Cat

My cat, my friend, who loves me always,
Especially when I feed her.
She's a fluffy, cuddly ball who loves to sleep all day,
When I come back from school she's still there,
Asleep on my bed,
In the evening she goes out in the darkness,
When she returns she brings me a present,
She drops a mouse at my feet purring contentedly.

Ellë Laming (8)
Holbrook Primary School, Ipswich

What Is?

What is pink? A raspberry is pink,
You can eat one within a blink.
What is blue? A blueberry is blue,
I like blueberries a lot too.
What is green? An apple is green,
The greenest thing you have ever seen.
What is red? A strawberry is red,
The taste just stays in your head.
What is yellow? A lemon is yellow,
But the taste is not mellow.
What is black? A blackcurrant is black,
It is so small, it can roll down a crack.
What is brown? An over ripe banana is brown,
They certainly make you frown.
What is orange? Of course an
Orange is just orange.

Georgie Harmer (9)
Holbrook Primary School, Ipswich

Star

I see a star shining in the sky,
Glowing and glittering up high,
I'm afraid it will fall,
Although I know it won't.
How does it stay up there?
I wish I could grab it,
It's a million miles away.
Even though it looks much less,
I'll have to leave it where it is.

Carys Todd (8)
Holbrook Primary School, Ipswich

Pets

Animals and insects, big or small,
As pets we like to have them all.
From small mice that play hide-and-seek,
To long hissing snakes all smooth and sleek.

Bugsy the rabbit who likes to munch carrot
And then there is Polly, the brightly coloured parrot.
Cats and kittens who like milk in their dish,
In a warm tank you can find our tropical fish.

Hamsters who go round and round in their wheel,
Guinea pigs who like to squeak and squeal.
Is it a stick or an insect - it's hard to tell,
A slow moving tortoise who hides in his shell.

Feeding and watering to be done every day,
Cages to be cleaned, even when I would rather play.
Looking after pets, there is always something to do,
My mum says it's just like living in a *zoo!*

Laura Wilding (8)
Holbrook Primary School, Ipswich

Animals

A nts are small and easy to squash,
N ewts like lizards are slippery and slimy,
I nsects are little and hide in a corner,
M ice get chased by cats that are fierce,
A ntelopes are like deer but are found in Africa,
L adybirds are cute with tiny black spots,
S quirrels are furry with long bushy tails.

Emily Sweeney (9)
Holbrook Primary School, Ipswich

My Mad Auntie

This is my mad auntie,
She has a pig called Snort,
She feeds him mashed banana
And wheaty bits of corn.

She puts lipstick on her nose,
Instead of on her lips,
She sprays perfume in her hair,
Smell it if you dare!

She reads books with missing pages
And sometimes upside down,
She irons with her toothbrush
And never gives a frown.

This is my mad auntie,
I think you can tell she's mad,
I must say she has her ways,
But I'm very, very glad.

Brontë Nicoll (8)
Holbrook Primary School, Ipswich

I Want To See A Dolphin

I want to see a dolphin
Swimming in the sea
Leaping, splashing, crashing,
Beautiful and free.

I want my children to see a dolphin,
Not caught up in a net,
But riding through the silvery waves,
A sight they won't forget.

I want my grandchildren to see a dolphin,
Not performing in a zoo,
But dancing in the clear, white ocean,
All shimmering and blue.

I want my great grandchildren to see a dolphin,
Jumping high into the sky,
Not a picture in a history book,
Showing how we let them die.

We need to save the dolphins,
Before they're gone without a trace,
For a world without a dolphin,
Would be a sadder, poorer place.

Keziah Green (8)
Holbrook Primary School, Ipswich

I've Been Swinging

I've been swinging
And swinging,
From tree
To tree.

Round and round
And I'm getting
Nowhere!
Definitely nowhere.

I am a monkey,
Going round and round,
I don't know where I'm going,
I don't, I don't, I don't.

But never fool a monkey,
As I already know,
I'm going round and round
And getting nowhere in all these tall trees.

Lucy Hall (8)
Holbrook Primary School, Ipswich

My Love To You

My love to you is like a shining star above my head,
The romance in the air is such a magnificent feeling,
It echoes in the whistling wind at night,
My love to you is a feeling no one else has experienced ever before,
My world is so far away from my love to you,
It is as if by magic my greatest dreams have come true,
My love to you is the greatest love in history,
Every time I see my love, my heart beats faster and faster,
I hear a song, a song which reminds me of you
My love to you is the greatest love in history.

Cherise Ramsey (11)
Kenilworth Primary School, Borehamwood

The Snow

Snow is white and sparkles like diamonds,
Snow is cold and powdery,
When it falls down, it is a snowflake.

You can make a snowman,
You can also have a snowball fight,
It is icy when it melts,
When you touch snow too much,
Your hands freeze and turn red.

See the pretty snowflake,
Falling from the sky,
Snow on the window ledges,
Snow on the bare branches.

Look into the garden,
Where is the green grass?
Covered by the snowflakes.
The beauty of the snow remains.

Namwinga Pakhati (11)
Kenilworth Primary School, Borehamwood

The Midnight Castle

Beware of the spiders,
As they crawl up the walls,
Beware of the dragon,
Watch his eyes burn with anger.

Watch as the spiders flee before it,
They are the dragon's slaves.
For them it's an honour
For us it's a curse.

The only way to break the curse,
Is to slay the dragon,
No villager who lives down below,
Has had the guts to go up there.

Carly Agnew (11)
Kenilworth Primary School, Borehamwood

My Poem

Roses are red, violets are blue,
You're the best teacher and I like you.
You are so pretty,
You are so kind,
A teacher like you is hard to find!

When we're in the classroom we have lots of fun,
You make the day seem like it's filled with the sun!
When we do our work you always make me laugh,
Even when we have to draw boring graphs,
Roses are red, violets are blue,
You're the best teacher and I like you.
You are so pretty,
You are so kind,
A teacher like you is hard to find!

Paige Kenny (10)
Kenilworth Primary School, Borehamwood

My Special Thing

Today I walked over the hedge to see
The biggest window ledge
I heard my friend say,
'Let's go and play somewhere over there.'

I turned around and there I found
The thing I wanted lying on the doorstep,
I was happy, I was sad,
I acted all bad.

When it shone, I said it was mine,
When it gleamed, it turned all mean,
That's why it was destroyed.

James Gething (11)
Kenilworth Primary School, Borehamwood

Talking

I'm very good at talking,
I do it all the time,
I don't know how I learnt to,
I'm glad it's not a crime!

I talk when I am walking,
I talk when I'm afraid,
I talk when with my friends,
It's a shame I don't get paid!

There are lots of things I'm good at,
But talking is the best!
Sometimes I get told off for it,
I am becoming a bit of a pest!

I talk when I am sleeping,
I talk when I am sad,
I talk when I am happy,
But when I talk too much though,
My mum gets really mad!

I'll never stop talking,
I'll never let it go,
I'll talk forever and ever,
Even when I talk real slow!

Amber-Rose Crossley (11)
Kenilworth Primary School, Borehamwood

Snow

Snow is slushy
Snow is mushy
It looks like whipped ice cream,
It's as cold as a freezer
And as soft as a baby's bum!

Ellie Kenny (9)
Kenilworth Primary School, Borehamwood

I Hate . . .

I hate poetry
I'd rather watch TV
I like The Bill and Casualty,
I can see myself on 'I'm a Celebrity . . .'

I hate homework
Math, science and literacy
They make me do it constantly.

I hate reading
I'd rather play with a pet
Everything you need to know will be on the net.

I hate teachers,
They always scratch their head,
It makes me wonder if they're dead.

I hate getting up,
It's too early in the morning
And normally it's pouring
Because school's so boring.

Stephanie Toull (11)
Kenilworth Primary School, Borehamwood

My Little Sister

My little sister is a pain in the bum,
She should of been a boy, she plays with a gun,
She always pretends to be a dog,
My little sister puts toilet roll down the bog.

My little sister has big blue eyes,
If she does something wrong she always lies,
She always tells Mum that it was me,
Then she asks if she wants some tea.

I would love to put my sister in a cannonball
And I don't want to see her until she is tall.

Shaunnie-Paige Borrett (11)
Kenilworth Primary School, Borehamwood

The Circus Lion

I saw a lion at the circus,
Jumping through burning hoops,
It made me wonder why and
Then I heard a roar of pain,
From the crying lion it came.

They clapped the keeper of the show,
But what they heard they didn't know,
The performing lion puffing with pain,
Thinking of the African plain.

Now the keeper
Mean as ever treating the lion
Like the African weather
But when he did the act I can tell you
He was horrible for a fact!

Jack Crawford (11)
Kenilworth Primary School, Borehamwood

How Sad It Is To Leave

It's time to leave,
I will be moving school,
I will be with new people,
I will miss all my friends.

I will always remember the good times,
I will leave the bad times,
I will remember all of the teachers,
I will keep all of the things people gave me.

I will thank all the teachers that taught me,
I will keep all of the work that I have done,
I will remember the games we played,
I will remember the fun I had at Kenilworth.

Chloe Tomkins (11)
Kenilworth Primary School, Borehamwood

Football

I went to the game to watch the match,
Our striker hit the ball so hard,
It was such a cracker for the keeper to catch,
It slipped through the keeper's hands so fast.

The crowd went wild as the players scored,
The excitement grew as they scored another,
The crowd roared, my friend and
I watched the match together.

The end of the game, we all clapped and cheered together,
The scores kept coming and made us happy,
We will remember the brilliant game forever,
I was so surprised when I got home
That we had won again!

Billy-Joe Beechey (11)
Kenilworth Primary School, Borehamwood

My Family

My family are my real best friends,
When I am alone, they're the first ones to be there,
I love them with all my heart
Because they're the ones who care.

My mum is my best friend out of them all
Because she has been there ever since,
I have been through good and bad times with her,
Maybe one day I'll become a prince.

That is one thing you have to think about,
Without a family you wouldn't be loved,
No one would be there for you,
So your family are very important.

Tanaka Beale (11)
Kenilworth Primary School, Borehamwood

Will It Be You?

I'm leaving school tomorrow, what will I do?
I'm scared about leaving school, who will help me, who?

I'm getting more frightened now, as the days go by,
I'm getting much more frightened now,
My fists are getting tighter now!

I will miss the school I'm at,
I really truly will!
I was told about a horrid new school
By my old aunt Lill!

I hope I like my new school,
I hope and hope and pray!
I'm getting a bit tearful now,
Is it the end of the day?

It is the end of the day now
I'm very sad it's true!
I'm very *very* sad now,
I think I need the loo!

I need someone who'll help me,
Will it be you?

Roseanne Chenery (11)
Kenilworth Primary School, Borehamwood

I Can Hear

I can hear swaying of grass,
I can hear the playing of brass.

I can hear some adults
Talking to each other.

I can hear a girl playing with her brother.

I can hear the birds whistling in the trees,
I can hear the buzzing of bees,
On one hot summer's day.

Samantha Judd (10)
Kenilworth Primary School, Borehamwood

Family

Family, they are always there for you,
Family, whenever you're down, they cheer you up,
Family, they're willing to do anything for you,
Family are special.

Family is feeling safe,
Family is one big hug,
Family means having your own space,
Family are special.

Family is fun,
Family means you're never lonely,
Family cares for your every need,
Family are special.

Family is having a laugh,
Family is playing games,
Family is going out together,
My family are special.

Daryl Joe Lambert (10)
Kenilworth Primary School, Borehamwood

Stars

Up in the sky scattered like diamonds,
Millions of miles away they twinkle,
Some say they are thousands of God's tears,
They're like sequins in a black velvet sky,
They've been there for millions of years.

All these strange and mysterious balls of fire,
Isn't it a really spectacular thing,
There's even a rhyme about them,
That nursery children sing.

Why do they sparkle millions of miles away?
Why do they fascinate us so?
How can they just be in the sky?
Maybe we'll never know.

Sarah Toull (11)
Kenilworth Primary School, Borehamwood

The Haunted Hospital

The patients in the hospital,
Falling off the beds,
Creepy noises at night,
Shadows in the darkness,
Patients sleep walking,
Falling down the stairs,
Windows opening by themselves,
Things getting lost, doors being left open,
People going missing in a week or two,
Less people shout, less people around,
Last year there was no one left,
Is that really weird?
I don't know what happened to them,
Do you?
Everything is haunted,
No one is even left
Today!

Daniella Villiers (10)
Kenilworth Primary School, Borehamwood

Let's Party

Party poppers, food and snacks,
Birthday cakes, presents and packs,
All those things, lots of fun,
Working with everyone.

Jumping up and down,
You could never have a frown,
Partying all night,
You could never get a fright.

You're always going mad,
Because they're all so bad,
Playing games, that's the best thing to do,
Winning prizes also too!

Lee Michael Woodhouse (11)
Kenilworth Primary School, Borehamwood

Snow Time!

Lights, camera, snow!

The snow is falling,
Light and heavy,
Snowmen are rising,
Snowballs are flying,
It's snow time!

Traffic crashing,
Loud and quiet,
Cold, blizzardy weather,
Icy slopes,
It's snow time!

Icicles dripping,
Drip, drop,
School's closing,
Sliding sleighs,
It's snow time!

Lights, camera, snow!

Jodie Reilly (8)
Kenilworth Primary School, Borehamwood

In The Snow

I woke up in the morning
And was told that it had snowed,
I found it hard to believe at first,
But checked and it was so.
I jumped for joy and raised my hand,
It looks like a layer of thin, white sand.
All glistening in the morning sun,
I knew it was going to be so much fun!
I ran outside all wrapped up warm
And built a snowman on the lawn.
But as the sun rose high that day,
It melted some of my snowman away!

Rianna Moule (11)
Kenilworth Primary School, Borehamwood

Football Poem

I don't mind,
When my fingers turn blue,
When I miss my bus
And I'm freezing through.

I don't mind,
When my face is green,
When I read about monsters,
Which I think I've seen.

I don't mind,
When my ears turn red,
When everyone stares
At something I said.

But I do mind,
When my boot flies off
And hits a player,
Where boys are soft . . .
Oh my God! I've been sent off!

Karl Bourne (11)
Kenilworth Primary School, Borehamwood

Shivering In The Snow

In the snow it is cold,
We are all shivering.

In the blizzard, it is freezing,
We are all shivering.

On the ice it is slippery,
We are all shivering.

On the snow, it goes crunch,
We are all shivering.

We are shivering!

Molly McDonagh (9)
Kenilworth Primary School, Borehamwood

In The Winter When It Snows

I like having snowball fights,
I like having snowmen,
I like making snow angels,
In the winter when it snows.

I always get icy hair,
I'm always very cold,
I'm always getting injuries,
In the winter when it snows.

I like it when there is no school,
I like it when there's blizzards,
I like it when there's lots of ice,
In the winter when it snows.

Oliver Bassil (8)
Kenilworth Primary School, Borehamwood

Why Can't It Snow All Year Round?

It's the time of the year
When snow has to fall,
No school, no nothing
Bore, bore, bore.

Lying in the snow making
Snow angels, getting a pile of snow
And throwing them at your friends!

Poor people stuck in traffic,
They don't know what to do,
At least we're having fun,
Just me and you!

I just love snow
Don't you?

Tala Sweiss (9)
Kenilworth Primary School, Borehamwood

I Love Snow

It's that time of year,
When it snow, snow, snows!
When you listen to the radio
And listen for your school to be closed.

With the snow so white,
Snowmen, snowmen, snowmen,
Snow angel's so white
And the cold, cold cold blizzard.

So white like a blanket!
No don't go away!
Oh no, it's stopped snowing!
Wow, it's come back again!

I love snow so much!

Leanne Murray (8)
Kenilworth Primary School, Borehamwood

Winter Wonderland

I love the snow, do you?
I love making snowballs and snowmen
And it makes me feel that
I'm in winter wonderland!

I always thought snow came at Christmas,
I love sitting at my window
And when it does
It makes me feel
I'm in winter wonderland!

Danielle Wesley (8)
Kenilworth Primary School, Borehamwood

Have Fun In The Snow

It's snowing hooray!
Time for fun,
So have a good time whilst you can
                Let it snow, let it snow, oh please snow!

Snow is like a white blanket,
No one should miss the chance to play in it,
Oh no! We can't go out anymore!
Wonderful, glorious snow,
Including snowmen and snowballs,
Now everyone is stuck in traffic!
Going home because school's are closed.
                Let it snow, let it snow, oh please snow!

Forever I wish it would snow,
Oh, yes we can go out!
Really, I'm having the time of my life!
                Let it snow, let it snow, oh please snow!

Lovely snow is falling,
Icicles dripping from my nose,
Forever, please let it snow,
Everyone's having a great time!

Having fun making snow angels
And hanging out with my friends,
Very quiet and peaceful out there,
Every day I wish it would snow,
Fun that's what I'm having,
Until night-time,
Never will I go home,
Let it snow, let it snow, oh please snow!
It's snowing for life! Have fun!

Hollie Coombes (9)
Kenilworth Primary School, Borehamwood

In The Snow In The Cold

In the snow, in the cold,
I see the wind blowing the snow
Into my face,
In different directions.

In the snow, in the cold,
The things you can do
In the snow.

In the wind, in the snow,
I make snow angels
And snowmen.

In the snow, in the cold,
The snow makes the world look clean
And Christmassy.

In the snow, in the cold,
The thing that's best of all
Is that *school* is *closed*.

In the snow, in the snow, in the cold,
You can stay outside all day long.

In the snow, in the cold,
I wish, I wish that it would snow on
Christmas Day.

Eleanor Marshall (9)
Kenilworth Primary School, Borehamwood

In The Shadows

It's getting late,
I've lost my way,
Why did I leave?
Why didn't I stay?

I look behind me,
Who's that? Who's there?
Just keep walking,
Pretend he's not there.

I start to run,
He's running too,
Why is he following?
What shall I do?

I'm scared but I turn,
What do I see?
It's only my shadow,
I was running from . . .

Me!

Lee Antony Lindsay (11)
Kenilworth Primary School, Borehamwood

Guess Who?

Fire breathing,
Kid stealing,
Mean and rough,
Hungry and tough,
Red with rage,
Escaped from cage,
Hero arrived,
Hero survived,
Sword in throat,
Dragon skin coat,
That's the end,
But will the families mend?

Katie Vest (10)
Little Gaddesden Primary School, Berkhamsted

The Three Little Wolves And The Big Bad Pig

You all know the story of the three little pigs,
Well this time it's different - the wolves are good,
There's a big bad pig, who's bigger than me,
Who lives alone in a little wood.

One day Mummy said to the wolves,
'It's time for you to leave,
Be careful and good in the outside world,
And keep out of the way of thieves.

So go and find a place to live,
Somewhere safe, maybe big,
With distance from the
The big bad pig.'

So the three little wolves,
Found somewhere to live,
But little did they know,
It was near the pig.

Piggy was upset,
They'd taken over his land,
They'd taken all of his food,
Except for the canned.

So the big bad pig said,
'I will get my own back,
On those three little wolves,
I'll catch them in a big, cloth sack.'

So the big, bad pig caught the wolves
And threw them in the river,
It made him feel good
And much, much bigger.

He'd got his revenge
And all his food back
And as for the wolves
They'd never come back!

Katherine Cannon (9)
Little Gaddesden Primary School, Berkhamsted

Robin Hood Gives To The Poor

There was once a man named Robin Hood,
Who had to go out and fight,
People thought he wasn't very brave,
On that dark winter night.

Robin Hood wasn't selfish,
It was King John who was
And Robin Hood had an admirer,
He wanted to marry her.

No one except Robin Hood would dare beat the king,
But when it came to the arrow contest,
The king would be fuming,
But Robin Hood knew he was best.

The poor thanked Robin Hood very much,
Now they didn't feel sad,
In fact they would never be sad again,
But Robin Hood turned bad.

Kate Rogers (11)
Little Gaddesden Primary School, Berkhamsted

Arcane

Long ago and far away,
In a tiny village in Hong Kong,
There lived a happy woman,
Her heart was full of song.

She was the world's best weaver,
Arcane is her name,
She was very selfish,
This is the story of her shame.

One day she was so selfish
She challenged Athena, a god,
Athena was the god of war,
But she always ate cod.

Athena and Arcane worked,
They carried on until the night,
The tapestry was finished,
Let's see if the judges chose right.

Thomas Gaden Nicholson
Little Gaddesden Primary School, Berkhamsted

Robin Hood

Do you know about Robin Hood?
If you don't you really should!
Why should I know about him?
Because he's more clever than the king!

Do you know about the merry men?
They had a hide out like a den!
Did they know Robin Hood?
They lived together, of course, they would!

Do you know about Friar Tuck?
He knew Robin just by luck,
Why was it lucky he knew Robin?
Because they met when he was robbing.

Do you know the tale of Robin Hood?
If you don't you really should!
It's the best, not the less
Get an arrow and put him to the test!

Harry Jeffersen-Perry (10)
Little Gaddesden Primary School, Berkhamsted

The Story Of Robin Hood

Long, long ago, in the times of old,
There lived an outlaw, brave and bold,
Feared by the bad and loved by the good,
He went by the name of Robin Hood.

In Sherwood Forest was his den,
Where he dwelt with his Merry Men,
With Friar Tuck and Little John,
They'd wander the forests all day long.

He fell in love with a beautiful maid,
In Robin's heart she always stayed,
She'd help the outlaws day and night,
With Marian they'd win every fight.

They stole from the rich and gave to the poor,
Defying the Sheriff and breaking the law,
Feared by the bad and loved by the good,
That's the story of Robin Hood.

Jennifer Cannon (11)
Little Gaddesden Primary School, Berkhamsted

Guess Who?

John hater,
His traitor,
Great stealer,
Good killer,
People lover,
Hidden cover,
Sherwood Forest,
Always honest,
Great archer,
Quick matcher,
Charming man,
Wonderful fans,
No laws,
Feeds poor,
Wears green,
Always keen.
Answer: Robin Hood

Stephen Berry (10)
Little Gaddesden Primary School, Berkhamsted

Robin Hood The Great

John hater,
His traitor,
Great stealer,
Good killer,
People lover,
Hidden caves,
Sherwood Forest,
Always honest,
Great archer,
Running faster,
Charming man,
Wonderful fans,
No law,
Feeds poor,
Always keen,
Wears green.

Jack Elkes (10)
Little Gaddesden Primary School, Berkhamsted

The Three Little Pigs

There was once three little pigs,
Who were moving away from their mother,
They were walking along the path together,
When the first little pig saw their father.

'May I have some of that straw?'
Said the first little pig,
'Yes of course,' and he gave him some straw,
He was so happy he danced a little jig.

The second pig saw a man with some wood,
'May I have some of your sticks,'
'Yes of course,' said the man and he gave him some,
He was so delighted, he did some football kicks.

The last pig saw a horse pulling some bricks,
'Hey horse may I have a few?'
'Yes young piggy take whatever you like,
Or if you want, I could take them for you.'

But the wolf ate the pigs with the straw and the wood,
Only the last one was clever,
He built his house so the wolf couldn't get in
And he lived forever and ever.

Laura Barthorpe (11)
Little Gaddesden Primary School, Berkhamsted

Captain Hook

Captain Hook
He was a pirate,
He was a crook!

His enemy was Peter Pan,
But this is about the pirate,
He thought he was 'the man!'

His only fear was the croc,
It had swallowed his watch,
Tick-tock, tick-tock.

Captain Hook had a crew,
Although they were such fools,
What is this?
Croc is here!
Help!
Captain is in two!

Eleanor Humphreys (10)
Little Gaddesden Primary School, Berkhamsted

Robin Hood

Dressed in green,
Hero, lover,
His enemy mean,
Better man than any other,
He's giving to the poor,
Gold galore.

Charming and strong,
He's never stopped robbing,
But he's never wrong,
Because he's Robin,
He always does his best,
He's better than the rest.

This is for Robin!
Hooray!

Georgia McCarthy (10)
Little Gaddesden Primary School, Berkhamsted

Three Little Pigs

Three little pigs,
Building their home,
Sad to leave their mother,
They cry and moan.

Three little pigs,
They all disagree,
On sharing their house,
They make them separately.

Three little pigs,
All have their way,
One gathers sticks,
One gets some hay.

Three little pigs,
The first very wise,
Gets some bricks,
Of which he buys.

Three little pigs,
Two in big danger,
Along comes the wolf,
Patrolling like a ranger.

Three little pigs,
But now only one,
Two are eaten,
The wolf weighs a ton.

One little pig,
His house strong as ever,
Wolf can't get through,
Never! Never! Never!

Sarah Hocking (10)
Little Gaddesden Primary School, Berkhamsted

The Three Little Wolves And The Big Bad Pig

You all know the story of three little pigs
This time it's different - the wolves are good,
There's a big bad pig - who's bigger than me!
Who lives in his deep dark wood.

One day Mummy said to the wolves,
'It's time for you to leave
Be careful and good out there,
And keep out the way of thieves.

'So go and find a place to live,
Somewhere that's safe and maybe big,
With a far distance from
The big bad pig!'

So the three little wolves,
Found somewhere to live,
But little did they know,
It was next to big bad pig.

Piggy was upset
They'd taken over his land,
They'd taken all his food,
Except for the canned.

So the big bad pig said,
'I'll get my own back,
On those three little wolves, some day!
I'll put them in a sack.'

So the pig caught the wolves
And threw them in the river,
It made him feel much better,
To see them bouncing in the river.

So he's got his revenge
And all his food back,
But as for the wolves
They'll never come back!

Rebekah Holden (10)
Little Gaddesden Primary School, Berkhamsted

Mythical Gods

Mythical Gods,
Can be mean,
Some people like them,
But I'm not so keen!

Shouting and raging,
On the hilltop,
Going red, all in a
Strop!

They can be peaceful,
Happy and wise,
Mercifully looking at us,
With their great eyes.

Now today,
We have our own Gods,
Some respect them,
Others think they're odd!

Heather Musgrave (10)
Little Gaddesden Primary School, Berkhamsted

The Wolf

Swift mover,
Silent hider,
Jungle grover,
Sharp teeth,
Hot underneath,
Fluffy tail,
Let's hail,
Creepy as a cheetah,
As focused as a fox.

Jack English (11)
Maldon Court Prep School, Maldon

A Wolf

I am grey
And I want to play
What am I?
I'm not that big,
I'll chew on a twig and pretend it is a bone,
I've got big teeth,
Just like my niece,
What am I?
I am a wolf!

Christopher Millidge (10)
Maldon Court Prep School, Maldon

Weary Wolf

Alert ears,
Beady eyes,
Swift as a snake,
Face like a fox,
Pounding through lakes,
Keeps on trying,
Carnivorous,
Deadly,
What am I?

Callum Bugler (11)
Maldon Court Prep School, Maldon

Tiger

Swift mover,
Jungle groover,
Animal skiver,
Bush diver,
No ones dinner,
De limber,
Tiger!

Cordelia Cumbers (10)
Maldon Court Prep School, Maldon

When Wolf Began

When wolf began he chose his teeth,
From knives of dreaded hell beneath.

When wolf began he took beetles two,
For eyes sharp and keen and true.

When wolf began he took his coat,
From the colour of a castle's moat.

When wolf began he took his feet,
Rhythmic like a drummer's beat.

When wolf began his legs were heather,
As swift and as silent as a feather.

When wolf began he attacked a sheep
And in drove his teeth, deep, deep, deep.

When wolf began he ran away
And while running he heard the farmer say,

'I swear by God, I swear by oath,
I'll shoot you, you great big oaf!'

Farmer went and got out his gun
And after wolf did he run.

When wolf ended the crack of the gun
And wolf was dead, the deed was done.

Joshua Carter (11)
Maldon Court Prep School, Maldon

Tiger

Tiger, tiger burning bright,
In the darkness of the night,
Claws slashing,
Teeth gnashing.

People screaming,
Children dreaming of what is to be . . .

James Baron (10)
Maldon Court Prep School, Maldon

Wolf

The wolf he has such sharp teeth,
His face looks friendly but beneath
His skin he hunts his prey,
During night and even day.

This wolf has a big long tail,
One full moon he begins to howl,
The wolf has alert ears,
This creature that mankind fears.

Rosie Coppin (11)
Maldon Court Prep School, Maldon

The Terrific Tiger

He crept like a cat,
He growled like a dog,
He roared like a lion.

His tufty tail twitched,
His jagged jaws jammed,
His colossal claws caught.

He howled the jungle down.

Alice Walder (11)
Maldon Court Prep School, Maldon

The Sly Tiger

Orange and stripy, the mastermind cat,
Snuffles round the corner for a meal or a snack,
The tiger finds a good hiding place next to a tree,
As sly as silver he stands like a statue not moving a whisker,
Bearing his teeth up and down,
He pounces with blood-red beady eyes,
But tiger is so vicious the meal was gone in one second flat.

Oliver Heward (10)
Maldon Court Prep School, Maldon

Wolf

A swift grey god,
Walks through the wood,
Hunting for his prey,
Listening for a rustle,
Ready to pounce,
Swift move caught.

Taking a meal back to his den,
Red meat, gnawing, chewing,
Wanting more,
Hungry cubs,
Hunting again.

Courtney Granger (11)
Maldon Court Prep School, Maldon

Tiger

Quick run
Here he comes
He's fast as lightning,
His stripes are frightening,
The king of the jungle.

Sharp claws,
Deadly roar,
Fiery eyes,
He is no boar,
He is a carnivore.

Jessica Quinlan (10)
Maldon Court Prep School, Maldon

Wolf Began

Wolf began
Through the forest he ran
As grey as dawn
He dines on fawn
His beady eyes alert
Wolf began.

Wolf began
He stalked toward the city of man,
His emerald eyes flashed in the sun
Paws moving one by one
He crept up on a flock of sheep
Upon a hill so steep,
Wolf began.

Wolf began,
Away from the sleeping man
He dragged his prize,
'Twas still alive,
He heard shouts and noise
A group of boys
With guns chased
Wolf began.

Wolf began,
The boys and a man
Followed wolf through the undergrowth
The man he swore an oath
A bang then pain,
Wolf ended.

Stephanie Baron (11)
Maldon Court Prep School, Maldon

Spirit Of Christmas

I was on my annual rounds,
Rushing in and out of houses,
To see what was there.
When I came to an enormous house
I entered to see what to see (I wish I had not)
What I saw was a disgrace
A boy yelling at his mother
For not giving him this, and that,
I did not like this for one minute
So I fled to an alley, there I saw
A girl wrapped in a small blanket,
I watched her for a while,
A man turned the corner,
He took out a carol book and said,
'Merry Christmas' she stood up and
Hugged him, she loved him, love!
This girl seemed to be living a
Better life than the boy.

Madeline Seifert (10)
Maltman's Green School, Gerrards Cross

City Lunch

Sitting watching mini-people rushing around
Pointing, staring, sitting on the girder
Gazing into the city.
The fear of falling off
That would be the end of me!
Sweating, waiting for this to be over,
Raised so high off the ground
Dreading to look down
Devouring, chomping, chewing, gulping,
Slowly eating.

Georgia Hanscott (10)
Maltman's Green School, Gerrards Cross

Colours

As I walked through the market
I did see;
Sapphire, bronze, scarlet, lilac
And many, many more.
I find that the colours remind me
Of a rainbow up in the sky;
There is strawberry red,
Rusty brown
And even a chrome and orange.
Each has its own basket,
Laid out on the floor
The colours,
The colours,
Are everywhere.

Emily Gravestock (10)
Maltman's Green School, Gerrards Cross

Colourful Scene

Dancing hues surrounded me
Lost in a world of colours
Extraordinary maroons, turquoises, ambers,
Tangerines, indigoes, crystals, limes, coffees and pitch
Blacks all gleaming in the sunshine.
Colours filled the atmosphere and turning
It into a multicoloured scene
Stall holders, coated with colours up
Their arms, in their hair, on their faces and up
Their legs, so beautiful, feeling as if you were
Just floating in the heating sun.

Leticia Baxter (11)
Maltman's Green School, Gerrards Cross

The Beauty Of Nepal's Market

Nepal's streets are seas of multicoloured powders
Drifting cloud like across the ground.
Above the dirt paths baskets filled with
Khaki, fawn, ochre and mocha,
Shades of red, strawberry, terracotta, crimson,
Blush, ruby and magenta.
Blues of every hue, sapphire, aquamarine, cyan, indigo,
Cobalt and navy.
Golden orb reflecting in the baskets of ginger,
Tangerine and peach.
More purples than Maltman's could ever imagine;
Mauve, plum, violet, lilac and lavender too.

Gemma North (11)
Maltman's Green School, Gerrards Cross

The Market

Mid-August
Everything is dry and dusty
The ground beneath my feet is terracotta
Dyes of a mixture of rainbow colours
Catch in the wind
I walk into the heart of the market
It smells wonderful, coffee, cherry and olive
The men who are selling fabric dye
Have it up their arms,
Turquoises, khaki, carmine, jet, moss-green
And opal
The market is colourful, alive.

Lara Shepherd (11)
Maltman's Green School, Gerrards Cross

High!

His acrobatic antics,
Raised above the city on the unfinished edifice.
Waving carelessly, no thoughts of fear,
Stoical builder stood, on top of the world,
How bold, how gallant, he is looked up to.

The vivid hammering of the hammers hitting the metal posts,
The echoing of the sharp, metallic noises,
Feeling comfortable above the rest.
No hazard, to him it is just how things flow,
It is no risk, it is just life.

To the builder, the people below are tiny dots,
To the people, the builder is *mad!*

Ayisha Gulati (10)
Maltman's Green School, Gerrards Cross

The Colours Of Nepal

Dusty ground of the Nepal market
Colours of fabric dyes
Merge into one before my eyes:
Auburn, red, crimson burn like fire before my eyes.
Sapphire, cobalt, azure, dazzling like seas.
Emerald, jade, forest, verdant,
Grass like the forests and valleys of cooler climates.
Golden, lemon, tawny, daffodil beam
Like the radiant sun in the sky.
Amber, tangerine, apricot mirroring the heavy heat.
Air filled with floating dust of the beautiful colours,
There on that day.

Kim Phillips-Page (10)
Maltman's Green School, Gerrards Cross

Colours

Black as a funeral, gloomy and inky,
it reminds me of a fireplace full of black sooty coal.
Brown as a plank of wood with streaks of beige,
as tall chestnut trees surround a beautiful garden.
Red, like blood, trickling from out of Jesus' wounds.
Roses with sparkling droplets in the sunshine.
Blue, like the water, sparkling in the sunlight
with the jumping, turquoise dolphins,
hiding in the roaring waves.
Bright, juicy, green grass for the rabbits to eat,
limes hanging from moss-covered trees.
Pink as a ripe grapefruit, sitting in a fluorescent pink bowl,
waiting to be tasted by our rosy tongues.
Yellow, the colour of the shimmering sun,
glistening in the aquamarine sky and below,
there is a gold treasure box, shining in the sunlight.
Orange, a colour that I adore, like a crackling fire,
warming up a cold, creamy, orange room.
I find all these colours above me in the glistening sky
with a bright rainbow.
Up above me, there are black and brown butterflies
surrounding me as I buy beautiful colours in the market.

Katrina Baxter (11)
Maltman's Green School, Gerrards Cross

Colours

Feet, dyed umber from the dusty earth underfoot,
A stallholder's arms covered in a myriad of colours
From the multicoloured dyes.

People carrying bags of vermilion, ultramarine,
Ebony, lush green, sun-yellow and plum.

Scent of spices fill the air,
Their colours conflicting for attention.

Hannah Dorkin (11)
Maltman's Green School, Gerrards Cross

A Raging Storm

Distressed, panicking sailors.
Hazardous, unyielding, wild wind.
Jagged, sharp rocks.
Aggressive, vicious storm.
Threatening, violent, powerful waves.
Tough, sturdy lighthouse.
Rushing, splashing, terrorising waters.
Terrified, worried lighthouse keeper.

Natasha Williams (9)
Maltman's Green School, Gerrards Cross

High Life

Dining in a perilous style
Substituting a girder for a floor.
Balancing precariously in the centre
Faith only in themselves and each other
Seemingly unaware of the crisis looming
Life below carrying on as usual
Simply four men eating and serving
Elevated in the sky.

Grace Joseph (10)
Maltman's Green School, Gerrards Cross

High!

Perfectly assured, not distressed
Waving, proud, in rapture to the camera
Stable, poised like an airborne statue

Wind whipping around his gleeful face
Practically soaring like an eagle
People below stand amazed and bewildered
Staring up at this brave fellow.

Amarantha Wells (10)
Maltman's Green School, Gerrards Cross

An Angel's Christmas

Once a year they carefully reveal me
From the old dusty tissue paper
Able to breathe at last
Waking into the angelic light
Yawning, stretching

I take a look at myself and realise I have aged
My burnished dress, so crumpled, so wrinkled
My crystalline wings in need of repair
My crooked halo, will they ever fix it
My curly, golden hair

Once a year I carefully watch
As the naked verdant green Norwegian fir is wheeled into the lounge
To be garnished, festooned, decorated and adorned
With the baubles, bells, tinsel and lights

The magnificent tree in all its splendour
With a vacant space at its pinnacle
I wonder if I am still worthy of the Christmas story?

Alicia Ptaszynska-Neophytou (11)
Maltman's Green School, Gerrards Cross

The Myriad Of Colours

Dry dust beneath my feet.
Bright colours surrounding; plums, citrons, titians.
Baskets of colours pushed together in neat little rows
ready to be sold.
Wind lazily blowing a myriad of colours softly across
the mocha ground.
Various smells, spices wafting up to the aquamarine sky.
Stallholders' arms smeared with chrome, blonde, jade,
ebony, bronze, crimson, rose and ruby.
Marmalade sun burning down on the crowds.
White clothes reflecting the rainbow display.

Gemma Samworth (11)
Maltman's Green School, Gerrards Cross

High

Pole balancing act,
Joyful, depression does not come his way.
Bold, feeling no pressure,
Lest he falls.

Traffic rumbling far below him,
Assurance always comes his way.
He sits with no thought of his peril,
Until the fall on his dying day.

Zoë Chambers (10)
Maltman's Green School, Gerrards Cross

Sea Storm

Large, violent sea,
Worrying, alarming night.
Robust, mighty wind,
Risky, hazardous storm.

Wild, threatening tempest,
Scared lighthouse keeper.
Terrified, panicking sailor,
Sturdy, tough lighthouse.

Charlotte Gilham (10)
Maltman's Green School, Gerrards Cross

Tempest Poem

Clouded, cheerless, dim sky
Violent, hazardous, tempest
Roaring, tempestuous water
Alarming, dreadful, petrifying terror
Destructive, defenceless, endangered lighthouse.

Shivani Patel (10)
Maltman's Green School, Gerrards Cross

Tempest

Violent, raging storm
Wild, ferocious, tempestuous sea
Hazardous, rugged, craggy rocks
Sturdy, strong, stocky lighthouse.

Tough, burly, fit mariners
Frightened, anxious survivors
Violent, harsh waters
Turbulent, boisterous ocean.

Gabriella Long (9)
Maltman's Green School, Gerrards Cross

The Storm

Wild, tempestuous storm,
Aggressive, violent, harsh waters,
Raucous, rough ocean,
Mighty, turbulent sea.

Brave, unconcerned mariners,
Distressed, panicking passengers,
Alarmed, worrying sailors,
Insecure, afraid survivors.

Clare Newell (10)
Maltman's Green School, Gerrards Cross

Tempest

Violent, aggressive, vicious storm.
Rough, hazardous waves.
Frightened, afraid, distressed sailors.
Robust, tough lighthouse.
Threatening, precarious rocks.
Turbulent, wild sea.
Powerful, alarming ocean.

Emily Eastwood (9)
Maltman's Green School, Gerrards Cross

The Tempest

Boisterous, raucous wind.
Wild, ferocious, tempestuous ocean.
Harsh, turbulent storm.
Hazardous, insecure rocks.
Aggressive, rough, mighty waves.

Threatening, powerful waters.
Encircled, robust, sturdy lighthouse.
Precarious, dangerous, unsafe.
Afraid, distressed mariners.
Endangered, alarming, uneasy experience.

Amabel Clark (10)
Maltman's Green School, Gerrards Cross

Tempest

A tough, mighty, boisterous sea,
Crashing against the hazardous rocks,
The violent, aggressive, vicious waves,
Encircling the sturdy, robust lighthouse.

Dismayed, faint-hearted mariners in awe,
Terrified of the treacherous sea,
Deep and powerful, tempestuous waters,
Furious, raging can ever be.

Alexandra Wiseman (10)
Maltman's Green School, Gerrards Cross

Tempest

Wild, hazardous winds
Fearful, scared, distressed sailors
Aggressive, robust storm
Violent, lively waters
Tough, encircled, solitary lighthouse
Faint hearted, endangered mariners.

Victoria Foden (10)
Maltman's Green School, Gerrards Cross

The Smuggler

Stepping with trepidation, ever alert for smugglers.
Silently it docks.
Prow becomes visible
Slowly the letters emerge
Letters become words
Gasping he reads:
'Smugglers' delight!'

Gasping suddenly -
Thieving from the crown!
Slowly he draws his rifle
Unexpectedly he is seen
Both fire
An uneven number remains on both sides.
Orange spots upon the sand
Where the blood and sand combine
Leaving a landmark and warning to all.

Emma Louise Goodey (11)
Maltman's Green School, Gerrards Cross

Colours

Beautiful, vivid colours make a tapestry of dyes,
Dancing exotic before your eyes,
Blues and sapphires are delightful hues,
Turquoise and greens evoke vivid scenes,
Mint and lime are shades divine,
Could my imagination have conjured up this collaboration?
Fiery reds, vermilion and scarlet
Tone down to orange, apricot and yellow,
Ochre, saffron, then shades more mellow,
Heliotrope, purple, lilac, lavender and mauve
All compete for life and creation.

Marie-Sophie Daniels (11)
Maltman's Green School, Gerrards Cross

Colours

Ruby-red like the glistening jewels in the cavernous mines.
Aquamarine-blue like the softly sighing Caribbean sea.
Silky chocolate like chocolate buttons.
Ebony-black like the chilled midnight hour.
Golden yellow like Easter chicks.
Orange like an amber necklace.
Emerald-green like sugar snap peas.
White like the cascade of a waterfall.
And last of all purple like the clouds of dusk.

Rebecca Dev (10)
Maltman's Green School, Gerrards Cross

Waves

Beautiful, alluring, dangerous,
Raucous, risky, precarious,
Fierce, insecure monsters.

Mighty, robust, horrific,
Tough, unyielding, sturdy,
Strong, powerful demons.

Lucy Tibble (9)
Maltman's Green School, Gerrards Cross

A Dangerous Storm

A mighty, powerful wind
Threatening hazardous waves
A turbulent, violent storm
The mariners panic and tremble
A raucous, aggressive storm
Endangered, alarming, uneasy experience.

Shabri Chandarana (9)
Maltman's Green School, Gerrards Cross

A Storm At Sea

Unyielding, dangerous, boisterous sea,
Mighty, powerful waves.
Unsafe, hazardous, rocks,
Strong, twisting, swirling wind.

Sturdy, firm, rigid lighthouse,
Robust, rusty boat.
Relentless, resolute gale,
Precarious, perilous, stranded survivors.

Samantha Foskett (10)
Maltman's Green School, Gerrards Cross

Smugglers

Riding through the dusky skies
In a dark midnight mask
Boats silently and swiftly going through the water
Police trooping down to the beach, taking out their pistols
Smugglers running out from the caves
Drawing their pistols as well
Then they start shooting and it is over
As soon as it starts.

Christina Osborne (11)
Maltman's Green School, Gerrards Cross

Christmas

Did you hear the bells jingling on Christmas Day?
Did you see the presents motionless on Christmas Day?
Did you see the tree sparkling on Christmas Day?
Christmas Day is a time to remember,
Full of happiness and joy.
Do not forget it's all about the birth of a baby boy.

Hayley Garnham (10)
Maltman's Green School, Gerrards Cross

The Smuggler

Mysterious smugglers
Magical, quiet, though alarming

Mystic sea, roars as he rides by
Moon glistens

Contraband is bought up onto the sand
Attentive guards in case they are caught

Resented and private
Contraband hidden in caves in cliffs

When the sun sets
A trail of hoof prints, all that is left.

Lydia Crawley (10)
Maltman's Green School, Gerrards Cross

The Smuggler

Shore lies waiting,
For the mysterious, magical man
Hiding in the shadows on that baffling night.
Dreadful, hair-raising, he now stands,
Waiting to attack!
Dark and spooky as he slivers secretly on his way

Charlotte Child (11)
Maltman's Green School, Gerrards Cross

The Storm

Distressed, panicking sailors
Harsh, raucous sea
Wild, enormous waves
Boisterous, unyielding waters
Mighty, vicious storm
Insecure, foreboding rocks.

Betty Makharinsky (10)
Maltman's Green School, Gerrards Cross

The Smugglers

Mystic man riding by
against the dark magical sky.
Boat, quietly docks,
men running towards it,
smuggling desirable, illegal goods.
Bloodcurdling noises of men being shot.
Then everything goes quiet.

Hannah Beattie (10)
Maltman's Green School, Gerrards Cross

Christmas

Glistening balls hanging from the Christmas tree,
Angel sits smiling at the top.
Presents waiting beneath the Christmas tree to be opened.
Santa and his reindeer clatter onto the roof, jingling bells.
Families rushing downstairs into the lounge.
Children gazing at the enormous tree, unable to wait until it is time.
Handing out shining wrapping parcels.
The glittering wrapping paper crying to be torn.

Zoë Kearley (10)
Maltman's Green School, Gerrards Cross

The Smuggler

Magical, quiet figure,
Creeping noiselessly
Across the sand
Alarming boats drift
Through misty fog
Secretly gathering their contraband
An eerie, blood-curdling scream
Suddenly comes out from nowhere.

Emily Baines (10)
Maltman's Green School, Gerrards Cross

This Is A Story

This is a story about a boy named Jack
and this is how he fell in a trap.
He went down town to pick a name,
for his new dog now called Shane.
He ran down the path to tell his mum,
he didn't know but he's rather dumb.
So he didn't see the construction pit,
with a loud *crash* he fell in it.
He went down a path,
then heard a mean laugh.
When he went to investigate,
he heard the crash of a plate.
He went through a doorway and saw a man,
just then a pole fell down with a great big *slam!*
He turned and ran until he could see,
daylight fading behind the trees.
He climbed out of the pit
and the sky was lit . . .
with the moon and one star,
he said to himself, 'Home isn't far.'
He was getting more tired
and he couldn't wait to sit by the warm fire.
He ran home as fast as he could,
but tripped on a pile of wood.
When he got home
he heard the phone
and heard his mother's voice say he's not home
he ran into the house (his mother needed to use a comb).
Just then he said,
'I will never leave home again, I will stay home instead.'

Toni Campbell (10)
Mundford CE VC Primary School, Thetford

The Boy Was Tea!

There once was a granny called Nanny,
Who had a grandson called Danny
They had a fox next door to them,
He guarded the tiniest of gems.
Now this wasn't a cunning fox,
No, instead of having a nice hat he had a horrible box.
Instead of having a clock inside this box
He kept the gems.
Now Danny wasn't a sweet little boy he didn't grow flowers with stems,
Instead he would chop them off,
He also had a horrible cough
And around his mouth he had some froth
From where he brushed his teeth that morning.
His granny gave him a little warning,
'Now before you go off to your hunting,
You will promise to stop grunting.'
He ran out the door and poised his arrow
And never saw the passage narrow.
Just enough to fit his body,
But before he could say Uncle Noddy,
The fox was out,
The fox had tea with Uncle Stout.
'That was nice my foul friend,
I need to go round the bend.'
Danny didn't come back that night,
Sometimes you can hear the fearsome fight!

Natalie Cosstick (10)
Mundford CE VC Primary School, Thetford

Curl

There once was a girl with a curl
Who always wore a pearl
She kept drinking fizzy
Until she was dizzy
And danced in a wonderful whirl.

Elouise Marenghi (11)
Mundford CE VC Primary School, Thetford

A Sweet Tooth For Cakes

A sweet tooth for cakes
I would do all it takes
Just to get one cake
But to bake a cake
It would just be too hard
When I have no lard
And no flour.
Without it, it would just taste too sour.

Chocolate and sweets
They're just not my thing
Cakes are the thing that make my tummy sing.
I don't mind chocolate
I don't mind strawberry
Just get me a cake because my stomach's in fury.
I would do all it takes
Just fill my sweet tooth for cakes.

Alexandra Summers (11)
Mundford CE VC Primary School, Thetford

Waves

Waves, waves, wondrous waves
Raging and roaring all day.

Splashing against the gigantic beach
Coming closer to the road all day.

Waves, waves, boring old waves
Doing the same thing every day.

Scott Palmer (11)
Mundford CE VC Primary School, Thetford

Jolly Roger

There are bones stuck right through its head,
its expression is grim and dead.

It brings fear to a merchant ship,
as it comes closer it makes happiness rip.

It is such an evil skull,
it is so evil and dull.

Its eyes are bottomless holes
they are blacker than pieces of coal.

Nothing survives it,
nothing escapes it.

Beware of the Jolly Roger.

Michael Brown (11)
Mundford CE VC Primary School, Thetford

The Consequences Of Battle

The clash of swords,
The shriek of men,
The twang of a bow string,
Could all mean the death of ten.

The swing of an axe,
The stab of a spear,
Could mean the difference
Between Heaven and here.

The defence of a sword,
The protection of a shield,
Could prevent dead bodies
Lying on the field.

Merrick Haglund (10)
Mundford CE VC Primary School, Thetford

Snow

Snow is falling
It is a warning
Whiter than anything you know
You are entering a snow zone
Making a snowman
Finding some buttons as quick as you can
Six inches deep
Under your feet
A snowball fight
At mine tonight
Walking in a winter wonderland
There is a snowstorm at hand
A carrot for the snowman's nose
As light goes
Going out in gloves, hat, scarf
Coming in to a hot bath.

Alice Dolton (9)
Mundford CE VC Primary School, Thetford

In The House

Once upon a time in an old, old house,
There lived a queen whose pet was a mouse,
Who lived all alone,
On his small throne,
Then he was eaten by a woodlouse.

The woodlouse's real name was Larry,
Who was a king, who wanted to marry.
He hated the sound of guns,
But loved to eat buns
And now he has a daughter called Carrie.

Georgia Morris (10)
Mundford CE VC Primary School, Thetford

Once Upon A Story Book

Once there lived a story book
And whenever the children had a look,
They were sucked into a magical land
And always landed in a pile of sand.
Last time when the children were there,
They saw a dragon kidnap a mayor.
They saw a knight without a care
And saw him ride into the dragon's lair.
The dragon's prisoners were tied to a post,
He had the mayor tied up the most.
Ladies and unicorns, all alike,
The dragon had stolen a brand new bike!
The knight came out without his horse!
The children saw the armour was coarse!
He jumped and bumped and fumed around,
Until he finally ran aground.
Then he caught sight of the children
And said, 'I have come to rescue Mildren,'
Again and again he pleaded for help,
Until he, at last, let out a yelp.
The children agreed,
But said they would need,
A couple of ropes.
He said he could cope.

Half an hour later they crept into the lair
And untied the town's mayor.
All the horses too,
The pigeons gave a soft coo.
They led them all out,
But heard a loud shout.
The knight went to rescue Mildren
And said, 'Thank the children.'
He set her free
And said, 'Come with me.'
They rode out,
The children gave a loud shout,
But unfortunately woke the dragon,
The people jumped into the wagon.

The dragon roared,
He caused a landslide and got stuck in the core
Of a volcano
And cried, out, 'Oh.'
Sadly the dragon died,
Nobody really cried.
At that point the children were sucked back,
With only the knight's horse's tack.

Kirsty Campbell Hibbs (10)
Mundford CE VC Primary School, Thetford

The Flea

Long, long ago,
Deep in the snow,
A bug called Terry,
Turned as red as a berry.

'So hot! So hot!' he cried as he fell,
His expression was mixed, you could not tell,
'What is it? What is it?' Mother bug cried,
'Oh no not again!' Father bug sighed.

'Mother, Father, it's my feet this time!
Help me out and I'll give you a dime.
Please, please! You must help me!
Oh no! Look! There's the flea!'

The flea was fat with skinny legs,
He had a big grin and gleaming white pegs,
He rolled on his tummy and licked Terry's feet,
The little fat flea had a delicious treat!

Terry's face went purple as he laughed with glee,
All because of a little fat flea,
The flea wasn't happy with all this screaming,
So he took his tongue and left Terry beaming.

Betsie Nelson (10)
Mundford CE VC Primary School, Thetford

The Robot

There once was an FBI robot,
Who saw President Kennedy get shot,
He chased the man,
Into the van,
Then the people said *he* was caught.

They brought him back to their base,
It was a fancy old place,
He rolled over his head
And saw under a bed,
A very big metal mace.

Cody Pumper (11)
Mundford CE VC Primary School, Thetford

No Gravy

There once was a young man in the navy
Who said, 'Oh no there's no gravy!'
He went to the shop
And off he did hop
And never returned with the gravy.

Paige Gooch (10)
Mundford CE VC Primary School, Thetford

Spoons

There once was a young boy from Troon,
Whose nose could balance a spoon,
But his mother said,
'Don't do it in bed,'
As he slept by the light of the moon.

Sam Rodé (10)
Mundford CE VC Primary School, Thetford

The Land Of Shandigoo

The land of Shandigoo,
The cows go oink instead of moo,
The cats have wings
And miaow at things,
But are put together with glue.

In the land of Shandigoo,
The people just wear one shoe,
With a pair of pants
And legs like ants,
They get around with just goo.

In the land of Shandigoo,
Everyone acts cuckoo,
With hats of straw
And arms galore,
That's the land of Shandigoo.

Benjamin Clark (10)
Mundford CE VC Primary School, Thetford

The Night

In the dim night
The stars shine incredibly.

Night is a big terror
Like a test error.

When it's cold and dark
You hear extremely deafening footsteps
On the bark.

When you're in your bedroom
When it turns to night,
You will have to be brave to
Not have a fright.

When you're in the moonlight
It is bright.

Blake Benjamin (11)
Myland Primary School, Colchester

Terrors Of The Night

In the night's sky the bats will fly
And the wolves sound their deadly cry.
The black cat runs away in fright
In the terrors of the night.

Thick branches stretch to me
From a fallen crumbled tree.
The vampires lurk about and they might
Get you in the terrors of the night.

As I hide under my bed,
Ouch, I just banged my head,
All is see is a freaky light
In the terrors of the night.

So if you're in
The terrors of the night,
Don't fool yourself
You're in for a fright.

Aimée Jade Artus (11)
Myland Primary School, Colchester

The Midnight Crime

In the depths of the night
A single lamp flickers light
As she walks unaware down the street.
A glance over her shoulder
Means at once she feels colder,
Then she listens to the creep of his feet.
She's silently weeping
As the neighbours are sleeping,
His breath sending shivers down her spine.
In his hand was the knife
That would soon take her life,
She was the victim of the midnight crime.

Lauren Humbles (11)
Myland Primary School, Colchester

Maths

Maths, maths
Makes me snore.
Maths, maths
Is such a bore,
All this silly revision
About multiplication and division
Really is a chore!

Maths, maths
What's three fifths divided by four?
Maths, maths,
My concentration's poor.
I have some bad reactions
To these pointless fractions!
I don't understand why school's a law!

Maths, maths
Makes me yell!
Maths, maths
It's a spell
To make me fall asleep
And shout and weep
And long to stick my head
Right through a solid brick wall!

Robert Beauchamp (11)
Myland Primary School, Colchester

In The Darkness Of The Night

In the darkness of the night
Is the moon shining bright,
With the flutter of the bats,
The twitter of the rats,
Floating around are the ghosts
In the darkness of the night.

Karl Lloyd (11)
Myland Primary School, Colchester

The Sea

The sea is a wonderful place
With the sea water on my face,
Fishes of all kinds
Swimming around at all times.

Octopuses with their eight legs,
Fishes laying their small eggs.
Sharks catching their prey,
A different one each and every day.

Jellyfish sting your feet,
A squid you wouldn't want to meet.
Sea horses playing with crabs,
Starfish gliding like cabs.

Seaweed's dark green,
Sharks are mean,
Oh! isn't the sea a wonderful place.

Heather Wald (11)
Myland Primary School, Colchester

The Sea

The sea is like a raging tiger
But can be as calm and smooth as a cat.
And you can hear the sea calling against the rocks,
Also it tastes like salty peanuts,
It smells like fresh squid.

The golden sand just lying on the beach
And the sunset on the sea.
When the sun is low you can see your reflection in the sea,
And when the sun is high,
There is fun in the sky.

Liam Eaton (11) & Keith Ajagun-Brauns (10)
Myland Primary School, Colchester

The Sea

The clouds build frantically,
Goodbye to the sun,
Ripples turn to crashing waves,
The ocean's having fun.

The sea plays catch with helpless boats,
Lightning reveals rain,
The murky waters swallow the beach,
A storm is here again.

Niall Rudd (11)
Myland Primary School, Colchester

The Sea

As I breathe in the fresh sea air
I look at the sea without a care.
I look over the calm ocean waves
And stare at the sunset and everything,
I'm thinking I seem to forget.

As the fish jump in and out of the waves
Under the sea are dark and abandoned caves!

Alice Bryant (11)
Myland Primary School, Colchester

Topsy-Turvy Poem

I wrapped up warm in the middle of summer.
I made an igloo when no snow was there.
I swam in a lake when no water was there.
The leaves fell off the tree, but where were they?
I put up my umbrella when it wasn't raining.
The sun was shining but it was hidden.

Lelan Spence (8)
Myland Primary School, Colchester

I Hate Maths!

Maths is so boring,
I hate every sum,
When I'm not snoring
My brain goes quite numb.

I hate long division
And reading the scale,
If we start revision,
I want to wail.

I envy the clever dude
Who starts to measure
The weight of the food
At his leisure.

After every digit
I drift away,
Beginning to fidget
And starting to play.

He starts to glare
At my blank face,
I start to stare
Up into space.

As the bell starts to sing
I leap from my chair,
The voices ring,
He holds me back, how unfair!

He says I'm a bad child,
I want to object,
His chastisement was mild,
I *hate* this subject.

Karthik Chandrasekharan (10)
Myland Primary School, Colchester

The Night

It will be a ghostly night
When some people might get a fright.
Dogs will endlessly bark
In the scary dark.
Soon the moon will rise again,
Here we will go all over again.

It will be a ghostly night
Until the morning light,
Where in the redness of the sky
The birds will fly.

It was a ghostly night
When some people got a terrible fright.

James Buckley (11)
Myland Primary School, Colchester

The Sea

The sea can be crashing
Or even bashing.

The sea can be calm
Causing no harm.

The sea can be rough
And very tough.

The sea can be silent
And also violent.

Yes the sea can be different in all ways,
But best of all I like sunny days.

Bethany Pike (11)
Myland Primary School, Colchester

The Night

In the silent night the moon is light,
With the stars all special,
And they fill the night sky,
Then it's broken by the morning light.

We wait a day
For the night to say,
I'm back again
With a dark blue sky
And night is my special name.

Izzy Sagnella (10)
Myland Primary School, Colchester

Topsy-Turvy Poem

I fed the rabbit when I didn't have one,
I put the light on when I was out,
I will give you a boat if you swim in the sea,
If you come in, then go away,
I pack my bags when I have no bags,
I cook marshmallows in the fridge,
I built a snowman in the summer.

Jessica Saunders (8)
Myland Primary School, Colchester

The Night

Silent at night on the calm beach,
Stars and moon twinkle,
No people there,
Just sand and water glistening,
Soundless but for the water's background humming.

Natascha Lopez (10)
Myland Primary School, Colchester

The Night

Night is a scary time,
I feel all alone in my foster home.

My teddy is made out of foam,
It reminds me of my real home.

The hours go oh so slowly,
I cannot sleep.

I lay on my pillow and weep and weep.
Why must I be here?
I don't understand.

From seeing my family
I have been banned.

Jade Basshier (11)
Myland Primary School, Colchester

The Sea

As the sun rises the sea is so calm,
The good tempered waves causing no harm,
It's pleasant and undisturbed, no people, no storm,
I'm relaxed on the beach, all cosy and warm.

It's later on, the wind's violent and loud,
The waves crashing under angry black clouds,
The wind rushing, blasting and blowing,
The waves rapidly, dangerously flowing.

It's pleasant and undisturbed, no people, no storm,
I'm relaxed on the beach, all cosy and warm,
Everything's peaceful not rough,
Of the sea, I can't get enough.

Helen Burt (11)
Myland Primary School, Colchester

Topsy-Turvy Poem

I went outside to watch TV.
I went to school when it was closed.
I turned the computer on when it was broken.
I planted a seed in the winter.
I toasted some toast in the fridge.
I saw a rabbit underground.
I had some dinner for breakfast.

Lewis Baker (7)
Myland Primary School, Colchester

Topsy-Turvy Poem

I drove my car and steered with my feet.
It was a sunny day but it was cold.
I turned the lights off so I could read.
I drunk my glass instead of my juice.
I went in the bath with no water.
I crawled to school with no knees.
I hated school with glee.

Sabastian Lever (7)
Myland Primary School, Colchester

The Night

It was a beautiful morning,
It was a splendid afternoon,
But when the night came in
It was not a pleasant sight.
The rain and thunder argued together
As the storm was getting harder and harder.

Jade Chenery (11)
Myland Primary School, Colchester

The Sea

In the sea where the fishes live
Is a home that no one can give.
As the waves go up and down
It always make me lose the frown.

Lots of visions are in my mind,
Swimming in the sea looking for what I can find.
The wind blows the sea air smells,
Relaxed and no cares I inspect the shells.

Dolphins diving to and fro
Just like before, long ago.
Now is the time I have to go,
The secrets of the night I'll always know.

Michelle Li (10)
Myland Primary School, Colchester

I Went To The Movies

I went to the movies to have a swim,
I went through the door when it was closed,
We watched the movie with no picture or sound,
The car broke but it kept going,
We took it to the garage when we took it home,
Mum opened the door when she locked it,
We turned on the light when it was summer,
We moved house when we were in our own,
I ate a snack when I wasn't hungry,
I went to school when it closed,
I read a book with no paper,
I went to bed when I didn't.

Hari Kaarthik Chokkalingam (8)
Myland Primary School, Colchester

Down Side Up

I went to the seaside when
I was at home.

I drank my mash
And ate my orange juice.

I was on my Game Boy
And I was dancing upside down.

I ate my pizza with a cup.

I got dressed while I was asleep.

Georgia Tokely (8)
Myland Primary School, Colchester

Topsy-Turvy Poems

I played football without a ball,
I put the light on so I couldn't see,
I turned the light off because I was scared of the dark,
I got a drink and there was nothing in it,
I was drawing a person without a pencil,
I went in the car when I walked,
I walked in the snow when there wasn't any,
I walked in the mud when it was grass.

Christopher Cooper (8)
Myland Primary School, Colchester

Topsy-Turvy Poem

I went to bed when I was wide awake,
I went to school while I was at home,
I turned the lights off to read at night,
I went to town when the shops were closed,
The man could see me when he was blind,
I touched the sun at night,
I walked down the stairs while I was going up.

Jordan Graham (8)
Myland Primary School, Colchester

Topsy-Turvy Poem

Today I went and got a drink from the club
When it was shut,
I saw a man that was not there,
I built a snowman in the summer,
I turned the light off because I'm afraid of the dark,
I hugged my brother because I hate him,
I read a book with the light off,
I'll give you a boat then you can swim,
I went to bed in the morning,
I told a lie when I told the truth,
I walked to school in the car,
I told my sister nothing.

Rhea Gopaul (8)
Myland Primary School, Colchester

Topsy-Turvy Poem

I brushed my teeth with the stairs,
I went into the hotel when it was closed,
I toasted marshmallows in the fridge,
I went to school when I stayed at home,
I put my umbrella up when the sun was out.

Gemma Willett (8)
Myland Primary School, Colchester

Topsy-Turvy Poem

I dreamed a dream while wide awake,
I stood on my head with my feet on the ground,
I put my umbrella up when the sun was out,
I drew a picture while sleeping,
I walked up the stairs while they weren't there.

Lauren Mott (7)
Myland Primary School, Colchester

The Spooky Castle

I get out of my house,
I go past the shop,
I find a black gate,
I go past the red flowers
And the creepy graves
Where dead people have been.
I see the big door,
I go inside.
I see a friendly ghost
And say, 'Boo,'
And find a fierce spider
On the box
In the robber's cellar
That has a lot of things.
I say, 'Scat,'
And it goes to the wicked web.
I open the terrible box
With rusty locks
I see the key to the castle.

Shaun Duplock
Old Heath Primary School, Colchester

I See A Song

I see a magical musician,
I see a flying fish,
I see sparkly stars,
I see plain planets,
I see a magnificent mermaid,
I see the biggest air balloon,
I see a shiny shell,
I see a rainy rainbow,
I see pretty patterns,
I see lots of lollipops,
I see fun flowers,
I see fantastic fireworks,
I see a musician bow.

Emily Evans (6)
Old Heath Primary School, Colchester

Kite Poem

My kite flies through the sky,
Speeding fast as I was dragged along
The smooth grass.
I feel the sky in my face,
I'm pulled along the grass,
The kite went higher and higher,
Then it stopped!
It hovered in the sky,
It nearly fell, but went really high.
I couldn't see it,
Then it came back down
With spins and twists and tricks.

Luke Murphy (9)
Priory School, Southend-on-Sea

Feelings

Loneliness is silver gleaming white,
It tastes like freezing, icy cold water on an arctic day,
It smells like nothing in a world of oblivion,
It looks like a room so white you can't see the walls,
It sounds like silence,
Loneliness feels like being alone on the top of Mount Everest.

Nervousness is the blackest black of blacks,
It tastes like saliva running down your red throat,
It smells like chlorine in a dirty swimming pool,
It looks like a pool of cold water that goes down forever,
It sounds like ear-piercing screaming in high-pitch,
Nervousness feels like butterflies in your stomach.

Proudness is a deep purple,
It tastes like cold vanilla ice cream on a hot day,
It smells like air in summer after it's been raining,
It looks like me scoring a goal in the last minute,
It sounds like people cheering loudly,
Proudness feels like being clapped at.

Joe Graham (11)
Roundwood Primary School, Harpenden

Anger

Anger is bold blood-dripping red,
Anger tastes like mouth burning,
Bone cringing vindaloo curry,
It feels like putting your hand in a raging,
Flickering, scorching fire,
It looks like your best friend going off with
Your worst enemy who's sneering horribly by,
It smells like toxic oil polluting the world
And spreading minute by minute,
It sounds like your screeching brother annoying
You while trying to do your homework.

Sophie Frost (10)
Roundwood Primary School, Harpenden

Roundwood Rappers!

The Roundwood Rappers,
Roundwood Rappers.

Pencil, pens, rulers too,
How do we survive, please give us a clue?

The Roundwood Rappers,
Roundwood Rappers.

Art, DT, science and maths,
When you're in Year 6, watch out for your SATS!

The Roundwood Rappers,
Roundwood Rappers.

Lessons all the time, no time for play,
We all wish the teachers would just go away.

The Roundwood Rappers,
Roundwood Rappers.

At the start of the day we can't wait to go home
'Cause all the teachers lecture us and moan!

Lucy Randall (10)
Roundwood Primary School, Harpenden

Winter's Curse

I see cruel icy hands of the lonely bare trees creeping towards me,
I sense the presence of shadowy creatures of the unknown tracing
My every movement,
I jump in panic as I hear the crunching noise of my own footsteps on
The leafy ground of the forest floor,
I tremble as the bitter frosty wind nips at my shivering fingertips,
I break into a run as I hear a rustling noise in the trees,
I feel a million eyes on me, watching, ready to pounce,
A blizzard whirls around me in circles, around and around and around,
I pull my coat tighter, shivering and shuddering,
As the trees close in on me
And I start to wonder if it's winter's curse.

Daniella Allard (10)
Roundwood Primary School, Harpenden

Dear Family

Dear Auntie,
Thanks for the lycra shorts,
Spotted yellow and pink.
Wow they're cool!
That's what my friends think.

Dear Uncle,
Thank you for the waterproof,
The rain just bounces off,
The hood comes out,
The zip goes up,
It's so warm it makes me splutter and cough.

Dear Grandad,
Thanks for the imagination book,
You can even go fishing
With the rubber hook.

Timothy Chisnall (11)
Roundwood Primary School, Harpenden

Rockin' Waterfall

Crash! Splash! Thrash! Smash!
The rippling waters crashing down, down!
Whack! Smack! Dip! Plunge!
The foam starts whirlpooling round, round!
Tumble! Fumble! Lashing and dashing!
Innocent leaves caught in the blow!
Gush! Splatter! Splat! Whisper!
The murmuring waters start hissing, hissing!
Splash! Drip! Dribble! Bang!
The rocks are crumbling, cracking, breaking!
Cold! Freezing! Icy and blue!
The rockin' waterfall is waiting for you!

Rebecca Cave (11)
Roundwood Primary School, Harpenden

Feelings

Anger
Anger is bright, bull raging red,
It tastes like burnt blackening toast,
It smells like cigar smoke slowly spinning round,
It looks like a scintillating orange, detonating volcano,
It sounds like a chainsaw slitting through your body,
It feels like sitting on a beach with burning,
Smouldering blistering sand.

Loneliness
Loneliness is the colour grey,
It tastes like ice-cold water on a bleak winter morning,
It smells like a neglected world with fumes everywhere,
It looks like a tramp wandering up a road,
Neglected by his family,
It sounds completely still, only the wind howling by,
It feels like fire inside you.

Dan Wells (10)
Roundwood Primary School, Harpenden

The Monsters

In the pitch-black moonlit night
All the monsters come out to fight.
They are big and small,
They are short and tall.
They are here and there,
They are everywhere.
They are fat and thin
With scaly skin,
With sharp teeth and an awful bite.
Don't be scared and full of fright,
You could be lucky, well you just might.

Thomas Kearns (10)
Roundwood Primary School, Harpenden

Mystery

I am an old mystic legend,
I survive for long centuries,
I resemble a young mare,
I am as white as snow,
I dance in your dreams,
I have hooves of silver,
I live in the sky
Above the tallest rainbow,
A singular horn bursts out of my forehead,
In the middle of the night when you're tucked up in bed
Look out of your window and you will see
Me, galloping by,
                in the sky.
                        Who am I?

A unicorn.

Sarah Hodge (11)
Roundwood Primary School, Harpenden

Emerge

A small egg
With no legs.

An edge cracked
It's just hatched.

A hungry eater
Getting bigger.

A crystallised ball
Up very tall.

A pretty sight
High up in flight.

Flying high
    A butterfly.

Tara Cornes (10)
Roundwood Primary School, Harpenden

Feelings

Happiness
Is a puddle of hope in a pavement of gloom,
A shining light amidst black rain of sorrow.
It is a spark of hope in permanent darkness.
Happiness is a flash of energy and joy
Like a whole new world, untouched by man.

Anger
Is a huge bright orange flame in a land of tranquillity,
White hot metal, yet still surviving at the bottom of the ocean,
A deadly bullet whizzing through a calm blue sky.
Anger is an exploding bomb propelled by rage
And vengeance, like a burning house.

Jealousy
Is a fluorescent green sword, attacking a world of calm,
A flashing bar of envy falling through a clear sky,
It is a deadly weapon of devastation,
Breaking up friends and turning them into enemies.
Jealousy is a jolt of hunger and greed,
Like a bucket of cyanide.

Sadness
Is a dark blue shadow in lights of eternity,
A patch of sorrow in a blanket of happiness.
It is a drop of pain in a cup of glory.
Sadness is a wave of despair and distress
Like a homeless child.

Theodore Green (10)
Roundwood Primary School, Harpenden

Anger

Anger tastes like blood-red, mouth-burning, hot chillies.
Anger smells like burning wood in a bonfire full of smoke.
Anger looks like the brightest flames of red in the Devil's lair.
Anger sounds like ear-piercing, deafening screams in your head.
Anger feels like you're in a boiling hot, steaming, fiery cooking pot.

Rory Williams (10)
Roundwood Primary School, Harpenden

Poem Rap

I love poems, I love poems!

Every day I write, write and write,
In the morning, afternoon and all through the night.

I love poems, I love poems!

You can do a poem about Jack and Jill,
Sit back, relax and take a chill pill.

I love poems, I love poems!

Poems can be fun, sad - anything!
Just write what you want, bling a bling, bling.

I love poems, I love poems!

So this is my poem, isn't it cool?
If you don't read this poem you'll be a fool.

I love poems, I love poems!

Olivia O'Neill (10)
Roundwood Primary School, Harpenden

Dream Come True

She has perky, pointy, alert ears,
She has a grey, sparkly, velvet muzzle,
She has a glowing silver body of baby soft fur,
She has a mane like flowing, pure silk,
She has a tail as wavy as the rippling sea,
She has hooves as shiny and as smooth as glass,
She has eyes as blue as a swimming pool,
She has eyelashes as curly as spaghetti in a bowl,
She has teeth as pearly as milky-white beads,
She has a tongue as pink as candyfloss,
She has a horn as strong as steel and rock,
She has wings as fragile as the thinnest thread,
She has an appetite as large as a double-decker bus,
She is a dream come true!
What is she?

A unicorn.

Charlotte Scott (10)
Roundwood Primary School, Harpenden

Season Haiku

Spring

Beautiful blossoms
Bright pinks and reds set the scene
Winter is no more.

Summer

The golden sun shines
Through the cherry tree's green leaves
Birds sing through the day.

Autumn

Creatures hibernate
Beautiful golden leaves fly
Life is at its best.

Winter

Snow pounding on roofs
Snowballs flying through the air
Christmas time is here.

Rory Scott (11)
Roundwood Primary School, Harpenden

Dragon Slayer

I walk across the dingy floor
And open a wooden, tattered door.
There he sits on a treasure hoard,
Preparing myself I draw my sword.
The wings suddenly pop up as if about to fly,
He opens a humongous eye.
He leaps at me like a bird of prey
About to bag his catch of the day.
I'm shoved against a gigantic wall
And land on the skeletons and all.
He starts to laugh with triumphant glee,
Then my sword pierces his scaly knee.
He lets out a mighty roar
And knocks me to the stony floor.
My sword is knocked from my bleeding hand,
With frantic feelings I manage to stand.
I run towards the rusty wood door
And grab my sword from the dusty floor.
Being an expert in combat art
I impale his mighty heart.
He bleeds and roars around the walls
And like a giant weight he falls.

Matthew Corcoran (10)
Roundwood Primary School, Harpenden

The Snakes

We're the snakes,
We're the snakes,
We eat the rats
And scare away the cats.
We're the snakes,
We're the snakes,
We live in the grass
And let the time pass.
We're the snakes,
We're the snakes,
We're the colour of the ground
And we never make a sound.
We're the snakes,
We're the snakes,
Our fangs are covered in venom,
They'll bite right through your denim.
We're the snakes,
We're the snakes,
A rattlesnake shakes
And can live in lakes.
We're the snakes,
We're the snakes,
We break our jaws just to swallow you whole
And it's just so easy to eat a mole.
We're the snakes,
We're the snakes.

James Gray (10)
Roundwood Primary School, Harpenden

The Dragon Rap

Once upon a time in a faraway land
A dragon rose up from the sand,
In the light of his sunglasses shone,
The little town was good as gone.

'I'm the most rapping dragon in the world,
I'll eat up all your boys and girls,
And anybody I shall find
Will really get a piece of my mind.'

He rapped his way through a dark, dark wood
To terrorise the neighbourhood,
And when he came across some meat
He stopped, bent down and began to eat.

He ate until he could eat no more,
Then, guess what the dragon saw?
A knight, in armour, standing there
Tossing back his golden hair.

The dragon was full, he could not eat
This knight, whose name was Groovy Pete,
So Groovy Pete chopped off his head,
Finally, the dragon was dead.

Bob Palmer (10)
Roundwood Primary School, Harpenden

What Am I?

A tiny tot,
A little dot.

Crack he's out,
The world he doubts.

A munch, crunch,
Too much for lunch.

He grows so big
And snaps a twig.

He makes a home,
All alone.

He's out of this place
To see the world's face.

I am a . . .
        butterfly!

Lucinda Scholey (11)
Roundwood Primary School, Harpenden

What Am I?

I play hide-and-seek,
At what I do I'm good,
I like to eat bugs
And so I should.

I use my tail to balance,
I see everywhere.
I live in hot climates
So my skin is bare . . .

What am I?

A chameleon.

Dominic Childs (11)
Roundwood Primary School, Harpenden

The . . . ?

A small white ball
That soon will grow tall.

A tiny head
That's very well fed.

A growing thing
To the branches will cling.

Going high
With its eyes will spy.

A tasty meal
That soon will feel.

Its powerful jaws
And very strong claws.

Its prey will be feeble
To the . . . eagle.

Greg Nelson (11)
Roundwood Primary School, Harpenden

The Boys

We're the boys,
We're the boys.

We run through the classroom
And shout and boom.

We're the boys,
We're the boys.

We strut through the playground
And we barge people around.

We're the boys,
We're the boys.

We run through the door
'Cause class is such a bore.

Christopher Featherstone (11)
Roundwood Primary School, Harpenden

The Rapping Playground Kids

We're the kids,
We're the kids.

We cause havoc wherever we go,
No teachers can stop us cause they're too slow.

We're the kids,
We're the kids.

We cover the walls with graffiti,
Usually while they're having their tea.

We're the kids,
We're the kids.

They suspend us all the time,
But is that really such a crime?

We're the kids,
We're the kids.

Dylan Hopkins (11)
Roundwood Primary School, Harpenden

Old Cars For Sale!

1982 caravan sister for sale, very big and bulky,
Can go quite fast but when it does it goes off in typical teenage stomp.
May need some repair but nothing a little make-up can't fix.
Has been known to break down as it's been out of breath,
But we will sell it for anything.

A 1950s dad for sale, very sporty and never runs out of energy,
But does have back and Achilles problems.
No petrol needed, only lager and beer needed to run.
Remember, never support Arsenal in this car
Or you'll be in for a crash.

A 1930s grandad for sale, in good condition but does have a big head.
He only goes 30mph as he has a limp in his left wheel.
He can be a bit annoying as he cracks up bad jokes all the time
But we will even give him away for free.

Samuel Rose (11)
Roundwood Primary School, Harpenden

The Birth Of Destruction

The sea rested as the day closed,
The beaches became empty as a swarm of clouds
Further blackened the darkening sky,
The sea rumbled as the tension was growing,
First, a bolt of lightning tore through the night,
The waves became bigger and lunged onto the terrified sand,
The worst of the annihilation was yet to come,
Ships at dock were jolted and tossed,
The sea galloped towards the golden sand
Not leaving anything alive in its path,
It seemed that God was raging and cursing the sea,
Destruction is born,
Rolls of thunder obliterate the sky,
Death is waiting to strike,
The mouth of the sea digested the fish and boats,
It calms down,
As the sky peeks its head out to see if the storm
Has exhausted itself,
Destruction is gone,
Never return,
All is calm . . . for now.

James Crosby (11)
St Aubyns Preparatory School, Woodford Green

Metaphors

What is . . . the wind?

The wind is the world sharing all of their secrets.
It is God blowing His love to all of His friends.
It is dead people's voices howling to the gleaming moon.
The wind is angels praying to God with their love.
It is God's voice introducing new laws to make the world wonderful.
The wind is animals communicating to each other.
It is devils discussing what to do with their prisoners.

Maria Ruffy (11)
St Aubyns Preparatory School, Woodford Green

The Harsh Sea

The blue, glistening sea smacks against
The beachy, rocky sand.
It is just like a dirty criminal being
Arrested by a policeman.

Terrified and fearful the sand shivers
Waiting for the rush of the waves to come.
All it could think to do is run away, but where?

The sand is even more terrified than ever,
The whole of its vision is a bolt of lightning,
All of the grains of sand virtually turned into a mini tornado.

Babies screeching at the top of their lungs
While their mothers panic and try to protect them.
The wild lightning is still as harsh as ever,
This must be a never-ending storm.

Let it stop,
Let it stop,
Let it stop . . .

Ammen Gill (11)
St Aubyns Preparatory School, Woodford Green

Christmas Poem

This is the weather snowmen like
And so do I,
When everyone hates to hike
And people start having mince pies,
And all the world goes to sleep,
When children go downstairs for a little peep
They find all their specially wrapped presents in a heap,
Their parents start to laugh and weep
And so do I.

Amelia Ruff (10)
St Aubyns Preparatory School, Woodford Green

Snow

We all were excited,
My sister's delighted.
So we head out the door
And our hearts are filled with awe.

We stamped on the snow
With a long way to go.
No need for a car,
But they follow the path.

We walked up the hill
With laughter so shrill.
When the snow is so deep
It's as white as a sheep.

When the snow gives a glare
It's as bright as a flare.
So winter is here,
Let's all give a cheer.

Freddie Sayer (10)
St Aubyns Preparatory School, Woodford Green

The Panther

The panther's eyes are mysterious
And its skin is silky black.
His paws are as sharp as a knife
And his bite deadly.
The panther strikes fiercely,
Biting his victim with piercing teeth.
In one second it is over
And the panther proudly clears up.
And finds another meal
To his satisfaction.

Jonathan Lalude (10)
St Aubyns Preparatory School, Woodford Green

Behind That Door

Behind that door
Is a violent volcano,
Storming and raging
Like the sea on the day
Of a whirlwind,
As it gushes down
To torment the humans!

Behind that door
Is a roaring, tenacious tiger,
Like the wailing siren
Of a crashing ambulance,
The teeth like stalactites and stalagmites,
As sharp as a razor!

Behind that door
Is the smoke from a dragon's guts
Steaming up the room,
Peering under the door,
Choking people who dare
To touch it,
It is made to kill!

Behind that door
Is the dagger,
The weapon of the midnight thief,
Abandoned from a war over,
The world behind the door,
His body sliced, chopped and splintered
Into infinite pieces,
He is dead!

Aditya Banerjee (11)
St Aubyns Preparatory School, Woodford Green

Droplet

I was a little droplet in the sea
Until the sun came out and lifted me,
I floated around above the trees and the ground,
Then I was pushed together with some of my friends
And we became a cloud without any end,
And we floated around for an hour or two,
Then I looked down and guess what I saw?
There were little toy houses on the floor,
With coloured ants crawling around.
We continued for a couple of days more,
Until suddenly I was dropped from my cloud
And turned up under the ground.
I crawled around under the ground
Until daylight I found,
I jumped out and guess what I found?
The sea, the sea, the sea,
And that's the end of my life's history!

Matthew Michell (10)
St Aubyns Preparatory School, Woodford Green

The Dreams I Dream

When I shut my eyes tight
And start to dream
I cannot explain
The dreams I dream.

Even if I fly over a mountain
Or steal a fountain
I cannot explain
The dreams I dream.

But then one day
I shut my eyes tight
And start to dream,
Now I can explain
The dreams I dream.

Leon Haxby (10)
St Aubyns Preparatory School, Woodford Green

Wish You Were Here . . .

Wish you were here
In the pale blue sky;
Where the fluffy clouds float
And the eagles fly.

Wish you were here
In the fresh countryside;
Where the foxes roam
And the water rats dive.

Wish you were here
In the dense forest green;
Where the grass grows wild
And the squirrels are unseen.

Wish you were here
On the highest cliff top;
Where no bird dares to fly
And soon all ears pop.

Wish you were here
On the golden seaside;
Where the sun beats down
And the seagulls glide.

Wish you were here
Right next to me;
Where you go, where I go,
And you see what I see.

Raymond Parkinson (10)
St Aubyns Preparatory School, Woodford Green

The Sea

The gentle surge of the sea
Edging to the rough seashore
Like a baby taking its first tentative step into the world.

As the wild, sea salt spray urges the sea
Side to side as it scrambles to the sandy surface,
Then it arrived.

The briny water cupped by the unruly gale
As it eroded the bay
Like icing sugar spread.

The turbulent sea water broke its containment
And into the calm world.

People laughing, skipping and dancing
Like crabs scuttling playfully.
Transformed gusts of winds which surrounded
The strong rocks with slicing knife-like precision.

Then the apocalypse is unleashed,
Showing God's wrath, menacing
Like a herd of raging Mexican bulls.

Laughter becomes cries of pain,
Skipping is now a run for their lives
And dancing is abandoned with no more time for fun.

Thunder devouring the bay
As it glides through searching for newly dead.

The sun almost slaughtered by the clouds
As it fights for its life.
All is quiet,
The storm lurks
Waiting to pounce,
Unknown . . .

Peter Joseph (11)
St Aubyns Preparatory School, Woodford Green

Creatures Of The Sea

A fin flicks in the gloom,
A scale shimmers silently,
A sword-shaped nose, out of the darkness, looms
And dives effortlessly out of reach.

A faint scuffle is heard,
A starfish skimming over sand,
As quickly as a bird
It buries itself discreetly.

A whale basks in the warm sun,
Rolling and twisting in pleasure,
He thrashes his tail, weighing a ton
And happily shoots water from his spout.

Beyond plays a dolphin,
Jumping and flipping in the air,
Flapping a silvery fin,
Gracefully diving beneath the waves.

So those are some of the many creatures
That the sea proudly features,
Do not wrack your brain and use specific lotions,
For I shall tell you that they were all in
    The Pacific Ocean!

Jennifer Shaw (10)
St Aubyns Preparatory School, Woodford Green

The Devil's Lair

The Devil's lair is inside my head,
Where fire blazes upon the stony ground,
And spreads until it reaches the precious Earth
And hits it with a lightning bolt while it eats away everything in its way,
Where snakes slither along the crumbling, half worn away ground until
They reach their master.

The Devil's lair is inside my head,
Where the Devil plans his evil schemes,
Along the dribbling blood he walks,
He drinks it with misleading pleasure and laughter,
The angels try to fly away but the bloody gas conceals them there.

The Devil's lair is inside my head,
Where magma explodes like a water balloon,
Grasping dominance over the now, lava covered Hell,
Where grimy muck seems admirable
And creeps around, looking for something clean to bite away.

The Devil's lair is inside my head,
Where souls reach out for me,
I cry for help but the unpleasant, echoing voices do not shout loud
Enough for me,
The Devil draws nearer and nearer to me,
As I scream after only a drop of life-taking lava drizzles down my neck
And I am almost a dead soul,
That is the Devil's lair.

Sameer Farooq (10)
St Aubyns Preparatory School, Woodford Green

Inside My Head

In the very mists of night
There are beady eyes in the distance,
There is a howling wind in the sky
And leaves flying past your feet
And dust blowing into your face.

In the very mists of night
An owl swoops down to catch its prey
And take it to its children.
The owl flies low and silent
Waiting for a chance to catch its prey.

In the very mists of night
A dog barks at a nearby cat,
The wolves howl at the moon,
The lions feast on two young deer
And the anteater devours a colony of ants.

In the very mists of night
The foxes run to their den,
The horses dash to their stables,
The dogs scurry to their kennels
And the hunters rest in their beds.

Mehmet-Can Akkaya (11)
St Aubyns Preparatory School, Woodford Green

Lonely Child

There is a lonely child in the far, far east,
He gives people a terrible scare,
With his fish-like scales
And his envied youth,
His only wish is to be normal.

He prowls and he mutters under his breath,
The very words that got him in this state,
For every child, a new day means joy,
But for this one, it means getting closer to death.

Binta Balogun (10)
St Aubyns Preparatory School, Woodford Green

Spring

Lambs skipping to and fro,
Butterflies sprinkled about.
Rabbits jumping up high,
Birds soaring through the air.
Flower buds opening up,
The sun shining bright.

The busy hum of the buzzing bees,
Grasshoppers leaping about.
Children playing with ladybirds,
Dogs barking at the excitement.
A gentle breeze goes through the air,
The shade of the big oak tree gratefully appreciated.

While the oak tree gazes at these sights
It sighs and wonders why winter and autumn have to come,
The snowy days when trees are neglected
And frost nips at the twigs and branches,
Slowly tearing away the leaves.

Aruna Pahwa (10)
St Aubyns Preparatory School, Woodford Green

Help Me

You make me mad,
I try to be nice
But you just don't help me
So I bang and stamp my feet,
Tearing out my hair,
Pacing up and down,
Cursing out loud,
Tears of frustration streaming down my cheeks,
Banging my fist on the table,
Kicking the air with a scowl on my face,
Gritting my teeth in agitation,
Please, please can you help me do my homework?

Mario Mastantuono ((9)
St Aubyns Preparatory School, Woodford Green

Inside My Head

There's an Armageddon
Inside my head,
Where blood spills
On to the floor,
Where driving blades
And stabbing spears
Kill, slice and sever.

There's an Armageddon
Inside my head,
Where kings despair
At the loss of their realm;
Where bodies are crushed
With righteous steel;
And armies smite the foes
Of their king.

There's an Armageddon
Inside my head,
Where the feral instincts of man become true
As they slay their foe with apparent glee;
And rivers and lakes are choked
With the bodies of the dead,
That is Armageddon.

Ross Partridge (11)
St Aubyns Preparatory School, Woodford Green

Snow

Snow is cold,
Snow is fun,
The snow is falling silently
And covers the ground like a blanket.

First tracks in the snow,
Marking out the way
Back to our warm home.

George Kingsley (7)
St Aubyns Preparatory School, Woodford Green

War

War is a painful
   Black,
It smells like decaying
   Corpses.
War gives an everlasting taste of
   Fear,
War sounds like the screeching of a
   Banshee.
War feels as sharp as a
   Spear
And as cold as
   Ice.
War's domain is the darkest depths of
   Hell,
War is a monster that will not
   Cease
Until it has fulfilled its destiny to wipe out the enemy's
   Life.

Harry Ellis-Grewal (10)
St Aubyns Preparatory School, Woodford Green

At The Seaside

The sea is gleaming bright as blue
and the seagulls are singing in the afternoon
under the brightness of the sun.

The children are playing with the sand
and shouting and screaming, just to have fun.
The sun is shining and it's very hot.
People go swimming in the sea and many boats go
steaming here and there.

Suddenly the sun changes its colour and gets ready to sleep.
It's night-time and people go back to their homes,
and the seagulls find their way home too.

Maisha Ali (8)
St Aubyns Preparatory School, Woodford Green

Behind That Door

Behind that door
Is a raging battle,
The bullets clanging like a pot being dropped on the floor,
The Devil himself would die of horror,
People dropping dead to the floor,
Cannons exploding in the heart of battle,
Men praying to live another day,
This is the bloodiest battle of all time.

Behind that door
Is the lair of the Devil,
The fire blazing like a petrol station on fire,
Magma spurting out of every wall,
The Devil drinking blood from his victims,
The eroding corpses stench filling the air,
The furniture is nothing but a stony rock heated
To one thousand degrees,
This is a despicable place.

Behind that door
Is the most sinister graveyard imaginable,
It is the very essence of the dead,
It contains the decaying bodies of every person who has ever lived,
It includes the souls of killers and murderers.

Christian Pannell (11)
St Aubyns Preparatory School, Woodford Green

Inside My Head

There is a deep, deep sea
Inside my head
Where the squids spurt ink,
Where tangly seaweed
Traps a passing fish
And smothers it into darkness.
Where the creatures whisper
In their unknown language.

There's a deep, deep sea
Inside my head
Where the jellyfish sting
Like pointy daggers,
Ferociously attacking their prey.
A shoal of fish glide past
Avoiding danger.

There's a deep, deep sea
Inside my head
Where moorfish are silver ghosts
Gliding through the sea.
An abandoned shipwreck
Lies at the bottom of the sea,
While coral grows steadily,
All different shades.

Emma Myers (10)
St Aubyns Preparatory School, Woodford Green

I'm Thinking

I'm thinking, I'm thinking,
I don't know what to write,
If I don't think of something fast
I'll be sitting here all night.
I've got to write a poem
Fourteen long lines long.
I still don't know what to write,
Now it's past 12 o'clock at night,
I'm thinking, I'm thinking,
I'll have to think some more.
I've written 10 lines all ready
Just thinking what to write,
Maybe if I think some more
I won't be here all night.

Bethany Lamb (8)
St Aubyns Preparatory School, Woodford Green

Fish

Fish come in all shapes
And sizes,
Different colours too.
Big ones, small ones,
Fat and thin ones,
Even the colour blue.

What a life a fish has,
Swimming all day long,
All around the seabed,
Blowing bubbles while singing a song.

When the evening comes along,
Fish find a place to rest
And only fish know where to go
Because fish are the *best!*

Gabriella Bloom (8)
St Aubyns Preparatory School, Woodford Green

I Am Me

I am me
You can't be me
You can try to be me
But you can't be me.

I am me
You can copy me
You can watch me
But you can't be me.

I am me
You can swim with me
You can play with me
But you can't be me.

I am me
You can have the same name as me
You can look like me
But you can't be me.

George Bayles (9)
St Aubyns Preparatory School, Woodford Green

Flower Power

Flower Power!
Purple, pink, blue, red . . .
Colour power!

Flower power!
Fresh from the bud,
Soft as silk.

Flower power!
They grow everywhere!
In your garden, fields, woods.

Flower power!
Smells so sweet,
Flower power!

Georgina Colton (9)
St Aubyns Preparatory School, Woodford Green

In The Dark Chilly Night

In the dark, chilly night,
the moon was dazzling bright,
the stars were twinkling like
real diamond rings.

The owls were wide awake,
while children were getting ready to sleep,
snuggled up in their beds
listening to their bedtime stories
with their teddies in their beds.

The moon had reached its peak,
the night was silent,
without a sound
while everybody was asleep.

This was the dark chilly night,
when the moon was dazzling bright,
the stars were twinkling like
real diamond rings.

Aisha Hussain (8)
St Aubyns Preparatory School, Woodford Green

The Funfair

Click, the car door opens,
I can smell the salty sea water,
I can hear the seagulls in the sky,
I can see the funfair from a distance,
Right next to us, people lie on muddy sand,
We head straight for the funfair,
Now we could hear screaming,
I knew we were going to have a fantastic day!

Sophie Roberts (9)
St Aubyns Preparatory School, Woodford Green

Toys

Toys are things that make you laugh,
you can play inside, outside and in the bath.
Toys are soft, squishy or hard,
toys cheer you up and can be your guard.
Some toys are ugly and scary,
some are pink like a small, thin fairy.
Some toys are big and some toys are small
and some of them are round like a ball.
Some make you laugh, some make you cry,
some make you giggle even if you're shy.
With some you fight battles against your chums,
Some make you closer to your dads and mums.
You get stretchy ones and slimy ones,
furry ones and grimy ones
Some of them squeak and some of them ding,
some of them honk and some of them sing.
Some of them smell like a sweet, ripe pear,
Some of the best are teddy bears.
You all have your favourites, I have mine,
You might like teddies but I like Bionicles in a line.

Harjay Singh Sehmi (9)
St Aubyns Preparatory School, Woodford Green

Snow

Silent and soft, the white snow came,
Landing softly on my windowpane,
Nice and fluffy,
Smooth and lovely,
The only enemy of the snow
Is the bright sun,
Disturbing our fun,
Slowly the snow melts away,
And where it once lay,
Lies the ice,
Tears fill my eyes.

Bomi Babalola (9)
St Aubyns Preparatory School, Woodford Green

The Four Seasons

In the spring the trees are blossoming,
The animals are waking up and the weather is getting warmer,
Everybody is looking forward to the summer.

In the summer, people like to go to the seaside,
They eat ice creams to cool down in the heat,
In the evenings you can smell the food from the barbecues.

In the autumn the leaves fall from trees,
Kids collect and play with conkers,
Everybody starts to wrap up warmly.

In the winter people enjoy playing in the snow,
Everyone looks forward to Christmas and the New Year,
When all the seasons will be repeated.

Haseeb Yusuf (9)
St Aubyns Preparatory School, Woodford Green

The Haunted House

Beware of the haunted house,
For you will be as scared as a mouse.
In the night it will give you a fright,
In the day it vanishes out of sight.

Monsters and vampires live in there,
Go in, if you dare.
The bats haunt the high, high heights,
Shadowing the ghastly moonlight.

The werewolves howl
As the air grows foul.
The ghosts float around
And one can't hear a sound.

Edward R Graves (10)
St Aubyns Preparatory School, Woodford Green

A Life Of A Snake In Captivity

Monday, feeling so homesick,
Tuesday, got beaten with a stick,
Wednesday, so bored,
Thursday, been ignored,
Friday, so tired,
Saturday, been admired,
Sunday, *fed up!*

Wild, I'm home,
Wild, I'm not alone,
Back to my relations
And lots of celebrations!
For lots of rats to eat,
And lots of juicy meat,
I am home at last!

Joseph Baum (10)
St Aubyns Preparatory School, Woodford Green

The Ballet Loving Builder

Charlie (or Charles to his friends)
Was a builder of skill and panache.
He carried his hod full to the brim
While elegantly grooming his moustache.

For Charlie (or Charles to his friends)
Was a dancer of flair and *pzazz*
Equally at ease with classic ballet
And down home and funky jazz.

His toe 'tector points
Pirouetted through the mud
And he laid all his bricks with a rhythm.
His feet were so light as he leapt round the site
That the rest of the builders leapt with him!

Gabriel Keegan (10)
St Aubyns Preparatory School, Woodford Green

Magic Box
(Based on 'Magic Box' by Kit Wright)

I will put in the box

Thunderous clashing of water upon the jagged end of the rocks,
Fire from the mouth of a red dragon spreading in the phosphorescent light,
Magic hairs from a white tiger giving me warmth whenever I need it.

I will put in the box

Three gold wishes spoken in ancient Latin,
A silver scale from a fish's silky body,
A lightning slash pouncing like a lion.

I will put in the box

The liquid of mercury running through the palms of my hand,
A yellow night and a black day
And stars made of steel.

I will put in the box

A pugnacious eagle feeding voraciously on its prey,
Lustrous snowflakes falling rapidly in the tempestuous fog,
A hellish lance coated with silky blood.

I will put in the box

A demon rising from Hell and an angel falling from Heaven,
A sanitised sword glimmering in the sunlight
And a snow mountain peak looking up to the moon.

My box is fashioned with a gold-plated window and a diamond-crested chain,
With a gleaming moon on the lid and a flash of silver coins in the corners.

Aaqib Anwar (11)
St Aubyns Preparatory School, Woodford Green

Snow

Snow is falling all around,
It covers everything on the ground.

With a soft, white blanket of cotton wool,
It makes the trees seem very tall.

Children go sledging on the hill,
They have to be careful or they will spill,

Out onto the cold and freezing snow,
That will make their faces glow!

The snowman stands so tall and proud,
Listening to the children loud.

As they throw snowballs in their fight,
Before home they go in the fading light.

Rachel Mortlock (7)
St Aubyns Preparatory School, Woodford Green

A Burglar In The Dark

Crash! In comes the burglar,
Ambling slowly into the house like a tortoise,
He cautiously opens a door,
He looks for valuables like a bear searching for food,
Finding two million pounds stored under a disused bed,
Suddenly the burglar alarm goes off,
It is like a death sentence to the burglar,
The burglar is as scared as a man about to be decapitated,
His family do not know that he is in a pitch-dark house,
About to be captured,
The police arrive like Formula 1 racers in their cars,
The burglar escapes just in time,
And creeps away like darkness itself.

Nicholas Dixon (11)
St Aubyns Preparatory School, Woodford Green

The Haunted House

Today I went to a haunted house,
When I went in, I was as scared as a mouse.
Then suddenly I heard a *whoosh,*
I ran outside and hid in a bush.

I had to go back, I had to see
What it was that had frightened me.
I opened the door with a terrible creak,
But it was the ghost that I had to seek.

I went upstairs into the smallest room,
In the wardrobe was a witch's broom.
No sign of a ghost, I couldn't find
What it was that was on my mind.

So into the cellar I dared to go,
There was a white figure with eyes aglow.
I looked behind at the shadowy shape
And found out it was just a white cape.

I ran away as fast as I could,
I ran and ran into the wood.
I'll never know if the ghost was real,
So I just went home to eat my meal.

James Carter (9)
St Aubyns Preparatory School, Woodford Green

Night Fight

You're cornered
Ready to fight
In the dark, still night
Fighting for what you love.

They're closing in,
Footsteps echo, echo
Through the dark night.
You stand there ready to fight.

Your heart is pounding,
Thumping, racing
In the cold, dark night
Where you stand ready to fight.

Your hands are clenched,
You're breathing fast,
Every sense is primed, alert
In the cold, still night.

Thomas Hartington (10)
St Aubyns Preparatory School, Woodford Green

Wind

It howls down the chimney, rustling the bushes outside.
Trees sway to the rhythm of the wind,
Lamp posts shake and the lights flicker.
The wind chivvies the clouds along,
The plane is battered by the swaying storm.
The wind whistles through my hair
Rough, freezing wind billows into my face
Nearly pushing me over.
White-topped waves are tossed by the wind
And crash on the shore.

Alexander Tudor (8)
St Aubyns Preparatory School, Woodford Green

The Dark And Gloomy Sky

In winter, the gloomy sky chases you
From tree to tree,
Rumbling and mumbling so loud and clear.
It sees you running and looking
For a place to hide,
But you can see nothing.

It sees you hiding in a little hole,
But you never know.
It catches you
And gobbles you up
And you're all gone,
So it's looking for another one!

Adara Wicaksono (9)
St Aubyns Preparatory School, Woodford Green

The Cheetah

I leap through the jungle,
My tail swerving round,
I prowl to catch my prey,
Not very easily found.

I'm the spotlight of the jungle,
And the fastest creature on Earth,
Unlike the laughing hyena
Who's full of mirth.

The lion thinks that he's the king,
The jaguar thinks that she's the queen,
But I rule this land,
For I'm the finest creature ever seen.

Isabel Roberts (8)
St Aubyns Preparatory School, Woodford Green

Paradise Zoo

I know of a small, private zoo,
I know it is near, but do you?
Here there are lions, tigers too,
Llamas, wolves and a kangaroo.

At night we hear the old baboon
Scream and shout at the golden moon,
The wolves howl and the meerkats peer,
Parrots squawk and the horses rear.

So many animals live in here,
Ostriches, tapirs, zebras and deer.
I love to wander between their pens
Watching them all make friends.

When I'm tired I stop for lunch
Then buy some bananas in a bunch,
These are for monkeys and apes
Who also like a few grapes.

Sophie Bishop (8)
St Aubyns Preparatory School, Woodford Green

The Snow

The weatherman said it's going to snow,
When it's coming, I don't know!
Monday morning it's not there,
Tuesday morning I get a scare.
My garden is covered in a blanket of snow,
Can't wait to get out, come on, let's go!
We make a snowman with a great big head.
Now it's time to go to bed.
The snow has gone, it's really sad,
My dad thought it was really bad.
I love the snow.
When will it be back? I don't know.

Sam Bromley (8)
St Aubyns Preparatory School, Woodford Green

The Match

Anything can happen,
We could win
Or lose.
The two captains and the referee
Make a decision.
The ball is kicked
And the match begins.

I find space,
Wait,
And call like a baby bird waiting to be fed.
Now it's flying towards me,
I position myself
And stop it!

Now I'm in control,
Because I'm small, I must fight to keep my prize.
I barge my way down the field
Glancing all around me.
Billy is there waiting,
I can breathe no more,
My heart is pounding in my chest,
One last, hard kick
And he has it.

My part is played,
The goal is scored,
Anything can happen,
And it does.
We win the match,
My heart is filled with joy.

Ben Wernick (9)
St Aubyns Preparatory School, Woodford Green

Carisa's Christmas Cracker

Carisa got a cracker
Yet to her surprise,
It happened to be empty
And there was no toy inside!

Despite the table full of food
And presents all around
Carisa made a sour face
And sat down on the ground.

Deep inside the cracker,
Instead of toy or joke,
There was a slip of paper
These words she read, then spoke:

'This cracker may be empty
It might have caused dismay
But count your many blessings
For some children got nothing today.'

She sat and wondered for a moment,
Ran her fingers through her hair,
Thinking, *Wouldn't it be better
If everyone would share?*

She smiled at her family
And counted everyone
For she did have many blessings
And a new Carisa had begun.

The cracker had seemed empty
But in it held some wise advice,
She was a lucky child and
In future she'd think twice!

Crichelle Brice (8)
St Aubyns Preparatory School, Woodford Green

The Day The Sun Stopped Shining

The day the sun stopped shining
Brightly in the sky
Now there will be no rainbow,
No rainbow way up high.

The day the sun stopped shining
Brightly in the sky,
Maybe it's a shadow,
It's stopped, I don't know why.

The day the sun stopped shining,
The flowers looked so dark,
The trees looked very spooky
And dogs began to bark.

The day the sun stopped shining,
Not a speck of light,
People were walking sadly
In the frightening light.

The day the sun stopped shining,
Animals snoring too,
Dogs and cats were sleeping
When the cows were going to moo!

Rhianne Saunders (9)
St Aubyns Preparatory School, Woodford Green

Behind That Door

Behind that door,
There is a vast wave kicking people's houses,
The volcano burning,
A slithering python as long as a tree,
Where scavenging rats flee,
A charging group of unicorns stamping on the ground,
The eagle charged down,
And raging tigers growl like trumpets.

Behind that door a wolf howls,
Falling stones trickle onto the ground,
Rain thunders down like an invasion of arrows,
The wind saunters through the dark forest,
Trickling stones snatch at people's hearts,
And crawling soldiers gasp for breath,
The wind treads its way through people's fences,
And lava enters a raging river.

Behind that door,
Someone is dying,
Earthquakes suck people underground,
A surging waterfall crashes on stones,
Diminutive dwarves enchant the forest,
And a colossal building touches the moon,
Reverberating howls pollute the silence,
And bears haunt a dingy forest.

Jack Drew (10)
St Aubyns Preparatory School, Woodford Green

I've Had This Shirt

I've had this shirt
That's covered in dirt
For years and years and years.

It used to be red,
But I wore it in bed
And it went grey
Cos I wore it all day
For years and years and years.

The arms fell off
In the Monday wash
And you can see my vest
Through the holes in my chest
For years and years and years.

As my shirt falls apart
I'll keep the bits
In a biscuit tin
On the mantelpiece
For years and years and years.

Nicole Barbour (9)
St Aubyns Preparatory School, Woodford Green

Birds

Birds swoop high
Birds swoop low
Birds fly fast
Birds fly slow
Birds can do a lot of things
I wish I had a pair of wings.

Owen Rees (8)
St Helen's Primary School, Ipswich

Earth/Nature

Soft soil, fresh flowers
Sparkling like a rainbow
People laughing in the sun
Having so much fun
Tree leaves fly in the air
People soaked through!
Woods hard like a volcano
Snow falls in the winter
Animals live in woods
Like ravens
Rain comes in the south
Runny mud makes a mess
People running in and out
From the woods
Making so much noise
Clouds fly in the storms
More people come to life
In the autumn breeze
People go on holidays
In the summer breeze.

Christopher Boyt (10)
St Helen's Primary School, Ipswich

Down In The Basement!

Down in the basement where nobody goes
there's a big, fat hippo picking his nose.
Down in the basement where nobody goes
there's a cheeky chimpanzee itching his smelly armpits.
Down in the basement where nobody goes
there's a fat worm wiggling around.
So never go down the basement!

Hannah Erin Turner (8)
St Helen's Primary School, Ipswich

Sadness

Bye-bye Dad,
Wish you were here,
Here's my tear,
Get back here.

I look at Mars,
I see all the stars,
With your face
On every bright one.

I hide my tears,
For you to be back here,
I need some space,
To get my peace,
Why can't you be back here?

Just as long as I think of you,
I'll be happy,
Hope you are too!

Hannah Barron (9)
St Helen's Primary School, Ipswich

The Day I Forgot My Homework

My teacher stretched her hand
Out on her wooden desk,
Pulled out a pile of homework.
I felt like running west.
My temperature dropped,
I lost the plot.
My head burst,
I thought I was cursed.
My face went red,
I should have stayed in bed.
Oh why is homework so hard?

Hannah Pugh (9)
St Helen's Primary School, Ipswich

Raindrops

Droplets of rain falling like gems
As white as fresh pearls
It makes oil spring to life
Holding colours of the rainbow
A veil of drips and blobs
Thousands, millions of them
Rain glittering in the sky
Like diamonds flying everywhere
Shining hail
Plummeting down
Quickly freezing your hands
Hits the trees with light
Makes them green as emeralds
Now the rain is pattering
No longer firing down.

Jethro Franklin (10)
St Helen's Primary School, Ipswich

Sweets

Sweets are lovely
And sweets are sweet
They are very good to eat
Drumsticks are chewy
And get stuck in my teeth
Boot laces are lovely to eat
Sprinkled with sugar just like I love
You know what my favourite sweets are
So I want to know about you
And your favourite sweets.

Louise Lear (10)
St Helen's Primary School, Ipswich

Weather - Good And Bad

Sun, scorching hot
Burning a lot
Giving us light
Ending night
A cloud like one feather
Heavy rain, unlike a feather
With lightning flashing
And also lashing
Thunder booming like a dog
Lost in the misty fog
With tornadoes whirling
And taking and hurling
Snow, great fun at night
It sparkles in moonlight
Hurricane, like an angry lad
This is the weather, good and bad.

Sean Johnson (9)
St Helen's Primary School, Ipswich

Dolphin

Silky
Wavy
Fishy
Dolphin
Jumping like a bouncy ball
Gently
Softly
Like a smooth sheet of metal
Make me feel happy and calm inside
Dolphin
Silky dolphin.

Emily Barron (11)
St Helen's Primary School, Ipswich

Changes

Rainforest,
Waterfalls,
Rain lashing down.

Magical,
Mystery,
Spirit everywhere.

Ice,
Cold,
Winter frozen leaves.

Fun,
Happy,
Sad, angry.

Fast,
Slow,
Leopard in the snow.

Moon,
Stars,
Birds singing sweet.

Jade Cavanagh (10)
St Helen's Primary School, Ipswich

Time

Built the universe,
Made civilisations die,
Is a master of peace,
Controls us all,
Fought our ancestors,
Polluted our planet,
Is a dangerous weapon,
Is victorious and strong,
Brought life to Earth.
It's time, yes,
Time.

Eleanor Turner (9)
St Helen's Primary School, Ipswich

Disaster

Tornadoes swirling, typhoons twirling
Earthquakes clattering, houses shattering

People screaming, children crying
People leaving, children dying
Volcanoes booming, tidal waves looming
Fire crackling, evil cackling

People fighting, children homeless
People arguing, children frightened

Evil is growing, faster and faster
This planet is a complete disaster

Disaster!

Hal Rudkin (10)
St Helen's Primary School, Ipswich

Earth And Its Nature

Misty fields
As dark as dawn
Cold and hot
When the weather is born
Rustling leaves
Green and brown
Hard and soft
Sharp and smooth
Flowers dying
Storms growing
Rivers, trees
Fresh air is . . .
Dirty as mud!

People don't care if it's clean or not!

George Tobin (10)
St Helen's Primary School, Ipswich

Chocolate!

It's everywhere in town,
You can eat it upside down.
It can be in different ways,
That's what my friend says.
'Come and try some!'
'OK!'
It doesn't make a sound,
No, not even bark!
But I know that it's definitely in the colour dark!
Some people think it's malicious,
But I think it's delicious!
And I'll tell you what it is,
Yes, yes, as quick as a whiz!
Chocolate!

Amber E Durrant (10)
St Helen's Primary School, Ipswich

Fire

Flames flickering,
Brightening darkness,
Buildings alight,
Killing people,
Colour flaming,
Wood burning,
Invincible light,
Gas sparkling,
Sparks dying,
Houses dissolving,
Destructive flames,
Son of the sun.

Henrik Anderson (9)
St Helen's Primary School, Ipswich

Nature

Sun says hello
Rain stays mellow.

Temperatures down
All over town.

Sun says bye
Hides in the sky.

Bees are dead
Off with their head.

Storms are coming
Hear them humming.

No one's out
Or walking about.

Clouds are changing
And rearranging.

How about all pollution
Do you have a simple solution?

The world is coming to an end
It's driving everybody round the bend!

Lauren Flood (10)
St Helen's Primary School, Ipswich

Disaster

Volcano erupts burning everything in its path,
Molten rock flying, only ash is left.
Icy blizzards freeze water, snow blocks doorways,
Hurricanes create chaos, sucking up monuments and people.
Tidal waves rush into cities, destroying buildings,
People run, they cannot escape.
Earthquakes split the land, separating families forever.
Acid rain burns trees, leaving nothing.
Sandstorms whirl around, sending everything flying.

Jacob Sharlott Sewell (9)
St Helen's Primary School, Ipswich

Twinkling Stars

There float the stars
To twinkle in the night sky
Golden dazzle angels are flying
Playing hide-and-seek

Moon is talking to the stars
Which are shimmering
Now all the stars are shining
And the moon has turned bright
Angels have stopped playing

So every time you are awake
Look out of your window
You might see an angel
Flowing like air.

Rukshana Aktar (10)
St Helen's Primary School, Ipswich

The Sea

Underneath the sparkling sea
Fish are swimming
With plenty of glee.

Above the cold, rough sea
People are playing
Having lots of fun.

Underneath the tropical sea
Corals are waving
And moving about.

Above the churning sea
People on the pier are having fun
Laughing and joking all the time!

Mhari Grant (10)
St Helen's Primary School, Ipswich

Journey's End

Gently gliding, paddle dipping
Water rippling, ears listening
Birds singing, flowers swaying
Sun blazing, shoulders burning
Water speeding, muscles working
A distant roaring, getting louder
Heartbeat racing, rapid breathing
Out of control, sudden panic
No going back, deafening roar
Gripping fear, falling, falling
Crashing, splashing, dropping, dropping
Rocks tearing, weeds tangling
Breath gasping, coughing, spluttering
Swimming, swimming, frantic swimming
Grabbing grass, pulling, climbing
Kayak bobbing, paddle floating
No hope of reaching . . .

Elaine Rees (11)
St Helen's Primary School, Ipswich

My Dog Billy

My dog is grey
He has a beard and barks loudly
He is the cutest dog in the world
That's what I think
He is so cuddly and adorable
That's what I think
My dog has chocolate-brown eyes
He has claws that scratch
And sniffing is what he does best
He's the best dog I ever had
That's what I think.

Georgina Anstee (9)
St Helen's Primary School, Ipswich

Storm

Sun hides,
Scared to show his face.
Dark clouds swarm overhead,
Children daren't go outside.
Trees creak and sway,
As the wind swirls through branches.

Rain as hard as metal,
Beats down on your back.
Hoods up,
Gloomy faces wonder when it will stop.

Thunder roars,
Lightning flashes!
Wind throttles branches,
Slowly, slowly.
Clouds drift off,
Water steams off pavements,
People laugh once again.
The storm dies.

Emma Williams (9)
St Helen's Primary School, Ipswich

Books

I love books.
My favourite is Tracey Beaker.
She's ever so funny,
Like a bowl full of jelly.
But now, she's like the witches.
The powerful boy is called Harry Potter,
He is the king of the Wizarding World.
I would love to be him for one day,
So I could disappear in the winter.
I love these books,
They are better than any other books.

Hannah Cotton (9)
St Helen's Primary School, Ipswich

Great, Great Garden

Out in the garden the sun just shines,
It's great, great weather.

Out in the garden the birds just chirp,
It's a great, great sound.

Out in the garden the grass is green,
It's a great, great sight.

Out in the garden the plants just grow,
It's a great, great colour.

Out in the garden summer never leaves,
It's a great, great time.

Out in the garden children just play,
It's a great, great picture.

Out in the garden the weather just changes,
It's great, great rain.

Out in the garden a rainbow appears,
It's a great, great colour.

Out in the garden!

Sangeeta Kaur (10)
St Helen's Primary School, Ipswich

The Bright Sunlight Fairy

My character is as brown as a burnt sausage
Her hair is as bright as sunlight
Her wings are as bright as red-hot fire
Her eyes are as blue as blueberries.

My character is as boring as a mouse with no cheese
My character flaps her wings all day
Like a bat in a night sky.

Chloe Etherington (9)
St Helen's Primary School, Ipswich

Fruit City

Apples plod around like builders
Mangoes dash about like postmen
Pears and guavas cruise around like Hell's Angels
And bananas dance around like clowns.

Oranges are walkers, sad and dismal
Peaches are celebrities, kind and cheerful
Satsumas are sportsmen, proud and concentrated
And tomatoes are businessmen, efficient and plain.

Plums are crowds of workers, toiling to exhaustion
Raspberries are journalists, researching with effort
Cherries are street slickers, prowling like cats
And grapes are policemen, marching about with satisfaction.

So when you eat another fruit, think of what they were -
A part of great significance
In the magical, enchanted, magnificent . . .
Fruit City.

Harry Smithson (10)
St Helen's Primary School, Ipswich

Disaster Growing

People dying, children suffering,
Soldiers killing, smoke spreading,
Animals bleeding, homes raided,
Hungry animals, torn clothes,
Bullets piercing, dirty gas,
Drains leaking, people living violently,
Foggy nights, tanks kill,
War, fighting, thunder striking,
Tornadoes twisting, comets dashing,
War is viscious.
That is disasters for the future or past, is it?

Marcus Kuzvinzwa (10)
St Helen's Primary School, Ipswich

Nature And Its Foes

Why is a butterfly called a butterfly?
As it has a lack of butter, but flutters like a nutter,
Should it not be called a flutterfly?

It is a bee for, can you not see, it has a stinger on its tail?
No, it is a wasp, for it is small and has a very distinctive wail.

The clouds of the skies can come in many different sizes,
It would be like a dream, with all its wonderful prizes.
How I do just wonder though, what it would be like up there?
With all of you and the humungous heavens to share.

But there is one thing that is not a prize:
The evolution and pollution!
With CFCs destroying the ozone layer all those animals will die.
Along with you and me!
The Earth sighs!
All systems will be shutdown.

In a couple of hundred years this might happen to Mother Earth
And all her children,
All the countries of our planet.
So don't spoil it for the generations after us,
Be kind to the Earth and she will be kind back!

William Johnson (9)
St Helen's Primary School, Ipswich

Nature

Soft snow, cold frost,
Sparkling like a star.
Fresh air, soft clouds,
Your cheeks are as cold as ice.
Hot sun, cool wind,
Changes like the rain.
Shining rainbow, bright flowers,
As delicate as the moonlit night.

Amy Forrester (9)
St Helen's Primary School, Ipswich

There Could Have Been Something . . .

Knowing the soft voice of someone you love,
Is better than being the best.
Keeping a promise,
For the rest of your life,
Is hard to forget.
Loving a person is
Hard to admit,
But you know some how,
You've already told them.
Telling the truth once in a while,
It's not right,
But there could have been something.
Sometimes you do things to save yourself,
When you're really saving much more than you expect.
Treating people with respect,
Is a lot more to some people,
But is a pity to somebody else.
Understanding that honest voice,
All above the rest,
Is really quite hard to do.
But in the end . . .
You're that person.

Rebecca Moore (11)
St Helen's Primary School, Ipswich

Fields With Leaves

A cloudy, indigo sky,
A sea-green fir tree
Which reaches the stars,
Sage grass whispers, 'It's really cold down here!'
Chocolate-brown branches full of bronze leaves,
Slowly, the wind rushes through
Fresh air flows.

Rujina Begum (10)
St Helen's Primary School, Ipswich

Weather

Cold, freezing ice,
Warm, hot sun.
Umbrellas coming to and fro,
Now the sun is hanging low.
People enjoying the park,
Suddenly it turns dark.
Again it turns
Cold, misty, wet.
Freezing, snowy, cold,
My life is just bold,
Like the weather is always told.

Emily Richards (10)
St Helen's Primary School, Ipswich

Space

Comets flying everywhere
Martians whizzing round
Black holes being formed
Satellites floating all around
Red super giants exploding
To create supernovas
Asteroid belt rotating
Between Mars and Jupiter
Space is infinite.

Stephen Caliguiri (9)
St Helen's Primary School, Ipswich

My Cousin Kane!

My cousin Kane is very messy
His favourite thing is watching telly
He likes his rolls with ham and cheese
Soup in a bowl is all he needs
He likes his chickens because they go *cluck, cluck!*
He goes to the park to feed the ducks
His favourite book is the Billy Goats Gruff
We read it ten times, and it's still not enough
He splashes in the puddles and gets water in his shoes
It's not because he's naughty, it's because he's only two!

Maisie Clarke (8)
St Helen's Primary School, Ipswich

It's Big And Blue

It's big and blue and just like you,
It sails through the ocean,
It crashes through the water, just roaming through,
When it's warned it jumps through the air,
No, he's definitely not like the mayor,
He soars through the water, yep just like you!
I know he is just big and blue,
He is normal like me and you,
Yep, it's only big and blue,
Excitement is him, just a big blue whale.

Hudson G Shoults (9)
St Helen's Primary School, Ipswich

A Crisp Christmas

Silent wishes filled the fresh, crisp air
Snowmen rang out happily for all to hear
Santa swept through the icy, delicate clouds
Holly sprang out of its hide and the rosy red berries trailed behind
The table was topped up with a delicious Christmas dinner
Icicles hung and dropped off frozen houses
Blizzards rested while snowflakes settled in their nests
Mary, Joseph and Jesus stepped with pride along the fragile street
Bells sang!

Lily Buckley (11)
St Helen's Primary School, Ipswich

My Mum

My mum is a 'do what you want to do after your homework' kind.
She is a 'buckle up for safety' kind.
She is a 'read you a story at bedtime' kind.
She's a
    Kind,
    Fabulous,
    Loveable kind.

My mum's a 'star in the sky that bring us light at night' kind.
She is a 'don't be late from school or your tea will be cold' kind.
She is a
    Caring,
    Sharing,
    Listening kind.

My mum is a 'tie your shoelace or you will fall' kind.
She is a 'breakfast is the most important meal of the day' kind.
She is a
    Sweet smelling,
    Loving, hugging,
    Rainbow in the sky kind.

And best of all, *she is mine, all mine.*

Tamsin Hurton (10)
St Luke's RC Primary School, Harlow

Animal Farm

Snakes that hiss
Tigers that roar
Down to the stables, horses galore
Rats that make people squeal
And hamsters that nipped me on the heel
Dogs that bite
Owls that come out at night
Fruit bats flying
Chihuahua screaming
Sounds like they're crying
Crocodiles are snapping
Splash, goes the milk
The cats are lapping
At the animal farm it's all going on, come on!
Before the animals are all gone

Karen O'Callaghan (10)
St Luke's RC Primary School, Harlow

My Treasure

I dropped my beautiful puzzle of mountains and sand
Now it lies in the ocean's hand
As it waits night and day
It looks excited on the bay.

As I swam to try and catch it
It did not like me a bit
But then a triangular point swam towards it
The shark ate it to bits.

After the shark ate it
The shark dropped down into the deep ocean
Now it is at the depths of the ocean.

Carla Mortimer (10)
St Luke's RC Primary School, Harlow

Oh Wonderful World

Oh world you are so good to me,
I just want to go out and roam you freely,
When I lie on your thick, green grass,
I feel like my life is just flowing past,
My love for you will forever last.

I love your streams and valleys high,
I love all the creatures in your sky,
I adore swimming in your clear, crystal streams,
I think about you in my dreams,
I feel I'm floating on a cloud of cream.

I sometimes wonder whether you are a planet or not,
I'd one day like to explore your seas in a little blue yacht,
Whenever I look into the sky I can see a smiling face,
I meet this joy and peace with embrace,
Oh I will treasure you forever with a smile on my face.

Jessica Beere (10)
St Luke's RC Primary School, Harlow

The Candy Store

Sweet, sweets, everywhere sweets,
Red, yellow and blue,
I love the sound of the yummy bubblegum chew,
All the candy, its sweet taste,
I don't like candy to go to waste.

Bubblegum, lollipops, mints and chews,
All to choose from - reds, yellows and blues,
Sweets, sweets, everywhere sweets
All to choose from,
Just for me and you.

Chad England (10)
St Luke's RC Primary School, Harlow

The Space Dream

As time goes on
Further and further
I wait until help gets nearer
I look at the world, small as an ant

I feel that space is my true place.

My failure and my success
Have led me here
I want to stay, I have no fear
No one can feel quite like I do

I feel that space is my true place.

And so they came
As time went by
It was a great to be up in the sky
Now I'm back and glad at that

But I still feel space is my true place.

Jack Doyle (11)
St Luke's RC Primary School, Harlow

My Brother

My brother is small and neat
He loves to eat lots of sweets
Big sweets, small sweets
He loves them all.

Chew, chew, chew
Go his teeth tucking into his gummy treats
My brother loves his sweets
I can't believe how much he eats!

Rakeem Dixon (10)
St Luke's RC Primary School, Harlow

The Countryside

The wind is blowing,
The crops are growing,
The trees are moving,
The sound is soothing,
The view here is just fine,
Nature, is so divine.

The feeling is extraordinary,
Now I feel even more caring,
I'm filled with happiness, love,
Joy, sent to me from above,
The flowers blooming, the grass green,
Who would want to leave this pretty scene?

Then the sky as if in pain,
Threw down many litres of rain,
The sound was nice, as the raindrops
Dripped on the grass and the crops,
The sky and clouds cried, cried, cried,
Tears gently dropping on the countryside.

Tom Juliff (10)
St Luke's RC Primary School, Harlow

My Guitar

I know I'm good at something when I play my guitar
I can forget my worries
Forget my teacher and everybody else
When I play my guitar.

When I play guitar
I'm in a different world
A place with music
That's where I want to be.

Emma Rogers (10)
St Luke's RC Primary School, Harlow

My Castle

On a cloud there's a castle
Waiting just for me
A castle with a happy laugh
Is where I want to be

Princesses with streaming hair
Magic folk skipping around
Unicorns running wild on rainbows
That is where I'll jump and bound

On a cloud there's a castle
Waiting there for me
A castle with a happy laugh
Is where I want to be.

Annie Groome (10)
St Luke's RC Primary School, Harlow

A Special Place

A special place is somewhere
That people go to think
A wonderful, calming place
It fills your soul with delight.

A special place can be anywhere
Somewhere peaceful and quiet
Or somewhere frightfully loud
As long as you feel at home.

But I would have to say
That my special place
Is within the warm and cosy feeling
That is my bed.

Jennifer O'Keeffe (11)
St Luke's RC Primary School, Harlow

I Love My Family

I love my family
They bring me joy
They look after me
And buy me toys.

I love my family
They are kind
Their touching smiles
Aren't hard to find.

I love my family
They feed me
And give me lots of drinks
And keep me healthy.

I love my family
They smile at me
They give presents
I love my family.

Kelly Lynch (10)
St Luke's RC Primary School, Harlow

My Family

They give me love
And give me joy
They give me more than they can afford
And when I have nothing at all
They buy me things and that is all.

They fill my heart with love and joy
My family can't design clothes
But they can give me my heart full of family joy.

Amy Jade Stean (10)
St Luke's RC Primary School, Harlow

Over By The Waterfall

Over by the waterfall is where I like to go,
Watching the water clash at the bottom and then it starts to flow.
By the waterfall there are flowers,
Pink, red, purple and blue,
They pull you in,
With their tender powers.
Over by the waterfall is where I like to go,
There are rainbows and the sun is shining,
It really shines and glows.
I like it by the waterfall,
It's peaceful,
I like it because the sound of the flowing water is graceful,
That's my special place,
Over by the waterfall.

Claire Pearman (10)
St Luke's RC Primary School, Harlow

Deep In The Forest

Deep in the forest,
Clouds all around,
Rainbow in the sky,
Sun shining down.

Ship sailing by,
On an open sea,
Past the rainbow,
It sails to thee.

Beauty and wonder,
Fills their tender hearts,
Exploding with glory,
And summer larks.

Tall, growing trees,
With colourful leaves,
Opening of buds,
Like Heaven above.

Feeling so special,
On top of the world,
Laughing with the daisies,
I'm in a magical spell.

Full with power,
And with light,
Smiling, playing,
Bliss, delight.

Natalie Bell (10)
St Luke's RC Primary School, Harlow

The Beautiful Sea

My favourite place is the sea
Sitting on the rocks
Close by the lock
I watch the sun as it sets
And listen to the waves
The closer they get.

When the wind passes by
I get a slight chill
Watching the sunset warms me up
I love the sea
With its great view of the sunset
It's a beautiful sight.

Shannon Molloy (10)
St Luke's RC Primary School, Harlow

On The Seaside

The seaside is my favourite place,
Seeing the birds fly by
Watching them make the letter V
It has to be a wonderful sight.

Standing on the hot sand
Making my feet burn and go red
Jumping around trying to get the heat from my feet
Is not the way it should be.

Looking at the dark blue sea
Watching the waves flow up and down
Seeing all the fish swimming
It has to be a wonderful sight.

Dalton Chamberlain (11)
St Luke's RC Primary School, Harlow

What Should I Do?

There was a young, handsome fighter
And Miss Muffet, he really liked her
Yes, you're right the one that gave her a fright
The fighter was so confused he had not a clue
What should he do?
He could think . . .
Whilst washing his hands in the sink
He decided to visit his Uncle Powers
He said, 'Why don't you give her flowers.'
The fighter thought he should just admit
But she wouldn't go out with such a twit,
'I've got it, that spider who sat down beside her
I'll go and I'll fetch him.'
He got on his horse and rode for days
But he got lost and went many different ways
That poor young fighter
He should have tried harder
But that wasn't the way to end
While stamping on the spider.

Georgia Souter (9)
St Luke's RC Primary School, Harlow

Grandad

When I am sad I'll go to him
When I am scared I'll talk to him
If I am alone
He's always there for me.

If I'm nice he will thank me
If I am helpful he will help me too
He is so loving to me
And to the rest of my family.

Louise Spiller (11)
St Luke's RC Primary School, Harlow

Butlins

The sky master is scary
Jacuzzi waters so bubbly
My party moves are great
The beat is fine
Sportsmanship is everywhere
Go-karting with the air in my hair

Coming down the slide
Running for the fresh air
Exercising, pumping iron
Feet getting stronger
Beach volleyball is fun
Entertainment from celebrities
My week at Butlins.

Eddie Njenga (10)
St Luke's RC Primary School, Harlow

Watching The Solar System

Standing by the window,
Looking at the stars,
I wish that I could count them,
But the distance is too far.

Full moon, waking moon, waving moon,
I watch them all with love.
Each one of them is different,
Shining from above.

As the morning starts again,
It is a shame to see,
The moon, the stars and darkness
All fade away in front of me.

Maria Lynch (11)
St Luke's RC Primary School, Harlow

My Place

There's a place I like to go
Where beautiful trees and flowers grow.

There's a place I like to go
Where people smile
And people pray
They sit on the grass and talk all day.

That place is not filled with silver or gold
But beautiful trees and colours so bold.

Whenever I'm there
I play all day
The sun comes out
And my cares are washed away.

Nicole Ray (10)
St Luke's RC Primary School, Harlow

The Rugby Poem

Rugby is fast,
Rugby is furious,
It is very much fun,
You get cold, you get muddy,
And that is what happens when you play the game rugby.

Ryan Melaugh (9)
St Luke's RC Primary School, Harlow

Sea Of Seas

Napoleon's boats calm and soft sailing across the sea
Sails made of silk and masts made of gold
The sea calm and soft
The wind and the air so strong and firm.

Jamie Dawson (10)
St Luke's RC Primary School, Harlow

Forgotten Land

Over a mountain faraway under a rainbow leprechauns play . . .
Around a tree trunk,
Hear the sound of water falling heavily to the ground,
Down, down, down the stream,
See fairies flutter with their crowns so bright,
And their cloaks shining with brilliant light,
To guide the way in darkest dreams,
The colour of magic this beautiful stream . . .
Through a waterfall,
Down a rock and to hear your mother call,
You'll come and play another day in this far forgotten land.
For now 'tis late and all is dark
The fairies play,
The dogs they bark,
It's time to sleep, not sit and stare at fireflies dancing in the
                                                      cold night air.
In my dreams I see them play,
I hear them sing, and through this I pray,
That I am blessed to always stand and dream
And inherit this far forgotten land.

Sarah Humphreys (10)
St Luke's RC Primary School, Harlow

The Wonderful Creation

I was sitting on the rocks where the sun sets
And listening to the waves, the closer it gets.
The wind is calm as it slowly flows
And the clouds moving as the time goes.
The sky is all colourful like a child's painting
And me watching the day go by sitting and waiting.
The day has ended now and the moon and stars are there
To create another creation for night-time everywhere.

Shannon Eley (11)
St Luke's RC Primary School, Harlow

Now Just Stop Asking Questions

'When will it be snowing?
Will I see the sun?
When will it be summer?
Will I see the rain?
When will it be spring?
Will I see the snow?'

'Yes dear, no dear
Now just stop asking questions.'

'When will it be my birthday?
Will I have a chocolate cake?
When will it be a holiday?
Will we go to Disneyland?
When will I have a bath?
Will I go to bed late?'

'Yes dear, no dear
Now just stop asking questions.'

Louisa Findell (10)
St Luke's RC Primary School, Harlow

Snow

S now is falling
N ice and cold
O n the ground
W hile people wait
M ake a big snowman
A nd a small snowball
N ow it melts.

Jordan Allen (9)
St Luke's RC Primary School, Harlow

The Italian Stallion

Riding across the sky,
His chariot of gold,
His horse of steel,
Glaring at the sky,
With a menacing look,
Hands hold the wrecking ball of Hell,
Swirling in the dark night,
He blazes his sword forward,
He cracks his whip of doom,
Suddenly lightning bolts from the sky,
Shaking the Earth,
A thrust from his fist,
Makes the clouds tremble in the sky,
Flash, sizzle,
The Italian stallion vanishes.

Mitchell Seymour (9)
St Luke's RC Primary School, Harlow

Snow

Snow, snow all around
Wherever I go, so much sound.
Children playing, having fun,
It will not end until the day is done.

Snow, snow everywhere
I want to go here
I want to go there.
So much to do on this snowy day
All my friends come out to play.

Snow, snow, all is white
So much to do like a snowball fight.
Such great weather we've had today
It will not end until it goes away.

Kirsty Hitchen (9)
St Luke's RC Primary School, Harlow

A Flame

A
flame
glowing,
dazzling your
eyes, it sparkles
like a star overcoming
your ice-cold heart. Dying to
fascinate you with its touch, burning
through anything in its wake. Glimmering,
leaping, dancing everywhere, its ever-changing
contours, swiftly flickering before you can blink.

Hayley Hughes (9)
St Luke's RC Primary School, Harlow

Dogs

I like to touch dogs
Their noses are as smooth as a frog's.
I like their waggy tails
And their claws are as sharp as nails.

Robert Millwaters (9)
St Luke's RC Primary School, Harlow

Rugby

Hard tackles on the pitch
Ram into players
Long kick, high kick
Offsides are given
Unbeatable team
Training hard
Yeah, we scored
Come on it's great man!

Ryan Matthew (10)
St Luke's RC Primary School, Harlow

My Dog Marble

My dog Marble,
Rolls along the floor
He likes you to rub his belly
And he likes bowls of jelly.

My dog Marble,
Is brown, black and fluffy
He has a friend called Buffy
And they know a duck called Duffy.

My dog Marble,
Likes to bark, shout and gargle
I love my dog Marble,
He's an absolute marvel!

Teresa Holdstock (10)
St Luke's RC Primary School, Harlow

Dolphins

Dolphins are funny
Because they can flick and kick
And don't get sick.
I asked my dolphin to do his trick
To do somersaults and impressive flicks and kicks,
Now he is older and still he does not get sick.

Megan Stent (9)
St Luke's RC Primary School, Harlow

Dogs

I love the softness of dogs,
But not when they itch themselves on logs
They're full of fluff and what's more
My favourite is a golden Labrador.

Eigdmear McCrudden (9)
St Luke's RC Primary School, Harlow

Dolphins

I love the way my dolphin flips
His impressive tricks
For soggy bits of fish
And never gets sick.

Now he is older and
Is very proud of his silky skin
That gets touched every day.

Lauren Luque (8)
St Luke's RC Primary School, Harlow

Fizzy

I love to touch the gooey, *fizzy* sweets,
Every time I taste the tasty *fizz*
I love the salt as I taste the *fizzy* sweet,
Every time you drink *fizzy* pop
It makes your mouth feel all tickly.
So soft, yet still when you drink it,
It goes up your nose and makes you sneeze.

Amy Bassett (8)
St Luke's RC Primary School, Harlow

Puppies

I love puppies
They are so warm
When I cuddle them
I am hot
And I get up
I love my puppies.

Rhianna Coulson (8)
St Luke's RC Primary School, Harlow

Puppies

Puppies are cute
They don't wear a suit
They are soft
Not hard as a rock
They can make you happy
They can make you say
They are cute
That's why I love them.

Khadijah Green (9)
St Luke's RC Primary School, Harlow

Dolphin

Little, little dolphin swim to me
You're smooth and silky to touch.
Your tongue is very rough
For catching food.
You do a trick in the air
You are fun to swim and play.

Helena Peppiatt (8)
St Luke's RC Primary School, Harlow

Cats

I love cats
They crawl in the night
I like cats' fur
It chills my hand
Keeps me warm
That's why I like cats.

Mollie Thomas (8)
St Luke's RC Primary School, Harlow

Fluffy And Gemini

Fluffy and Gemini
Lovely, sweet as can be
Bunnies cute and sweet
Best of all I love them.
They are my rabbits
I love the way they come to kiss me
And when they lay in my arms
Sweet, sweet Fluffy and Gemini.

Daniel Lloyd (9)
St Luke's RC Primary School, Harlow

Dog's Fur

My dog's fur is soft
And cuddly too.
It is warm and smooth
And nice and fluffy.
I love dog's fur.

Daniella Parr (9)
St Luke's RC Primary School, Harlow

Dolphins

Little, little dolphins
Swim to your friends
Don't be shy
When you touch the dolphin's head
Silky it is
Bye-bye.

Charlie Kiernan (9)
St Luke's RC Primary School, Harlow

The River

I always stay beside the river,
For me it is better than gold or silver.
The beautiful water carrying bubbles,
But people give rivers troubles.

I wish it could stop,
People making litter drop.
I hope people start to care,
Instead of standing there.

Peitro Randazzo (11)
St Luke's RC Primary School, Harlow

I Love Dogs

I love dogs
They're so furry and warm
Like a radiator
Always moving
Like a car
Fluffy, cosy
You should get one too.

Daniel Munden (9)
St Luke's RC Primary School, Harlow

Drool

I hate to touch drool
All wet and slobbery
Sickening liquid
Dripping from an animal's mouth.

Matthew Addicott (8)
St Luke's RC Primary School, Harlow

Finger, Finger

Finger, finger,
Poke everyone.
Finger, finger,
Catch everyone.
Finger, finger,
Do it for fun.
Finger, finger,
One for everyone.

Daniel Jackson (8)
St Luke's RC Primary School, Harlow

Kittens

Little soft kittens, cosy in my hand
Ever so cuddly, warm and tanned.
When you are older, you will be so fluffy
But just right now, you are ever so puffy.
Little soft kitten, can you come home?
I miss your fur so very, very warm.

Nicola Beere (8)
St Luke's RC Primary School, Harlow

Snow

Snow is fluffy,
Snow is cold,
Snow is puffy,
I've been told
It can give you a fright
In a snowball fight.

Conor Molloy (9)
St Luke's RC Primary School, Harlow

Respect

Animals are cute and also very kind
And some of them can even guide
Like a dog, fish or a bird
They are soft so I have heard
I have a rabbit, three fish too
And this is what I love to say to you
Animals are cute, they deserve
. . . Respect from you!

Ruth Nulty (8)
St Luke's RC Primary School, Harlow

Dogs' Noses

Dogs' noses are wet
Dogs' noses are fluffy
I love dogs' noses
They are cuddly
Cold, smooth and squishy
I love dogs' noses.

Matthew Browne (9)
St Luke's RC Primary School, Harlow

Winter Wonderland

Children gliding across the snow,
Having massive snowball fights.

I'm a bright, white blanket,
The sun is shining upon me making me glisten like silk.

I feel soft and fluffy,
I'm very crunchy, bumpy and crumbly.

It makes me very excited,
Playing in the snow.

Michael Jeffery (10)
The Bishops' CE & RC Primary School, Chelmsford

A Snowy Day

A snowy day
Children play.

We're allowed to go outside
Everyone loves to glide.

Playing in the snow
Teachers tell us to go.

When it snows, it is cool
We can play ice football.

Snow is fun
For everyone.

Snowball fight
In the night.

Time to go to bed
Rest your head.

Lucy Kirkby (10)
The Bishops' CE & RC Primary School, Chelmsford

What Am I?

I'm chilly if you touch me
I'm crunchy if you step on me
I glisten and sparkle in the sun
I'm soft, hard and fun.

I'm slippy and slidy and also very icy
You can build all sorts of things from me
I'm cold to your tongue with no flavour
I look like a thick white blanket.

Can you guess what I am?
I'm snow at wintertime.

Lauren Gillingham (10)
The Bishops' CE & RC Primary School, Chelmsford

Snowy Days

Snow is falling,
Children playing,
People laughing,
Excited people all around.

Tops of trees look like fairy cakes,
Snow is falling all around.

Snow sparkling in the misty distance,
Snow is still falling all around.

People slipping on the ice,
Snow is still falling all around.

Excited children making funny snowmen,
Snow is still falling, but slowing down.

Parents pushing children on a sledge,
Snow is starting to stop.

Children starting to cry,
The snow has melted away.

Emily Nicholls (10)
The Bishops' CE & RC Primary School, Chelmsford

The One And Only Snow

The crunchy snow filling the grass
Makes it look like a white blanket.
The lamp posts lighting up the snow as it falls.
At last the snow has come again.
The slushy, white snow crackling softly,
Landing on the ground.
When you touch the snow your hands are tingling
Shake it off!
The sun is shining on the snow
Making it shine from time to time.

Thomas Storkey (10)
The Bishops' CE & RC Primary School, Chelmsford

What Am I?

Look at it fall,
Look at it right over the mall.

Look at it drop,
Look at it hop right off that mop.

Look at the snowflakes fall down to the ground,
Look at me turning, twisting all around.

Look, I am hail,
Look at me, I am rather pale.

I look like a fairy cake when I land on trees,
I can freeze the trees.

When I drop I sparkle a lot,
Even though I'm not that hot.

I am the one, the only, almighty snow,
Stopping people from where they want to go.

Nathanael Rogers (10)
The Bishops' CE & RC Primary School, Chelmsford

When It Snowed

When I looked out of the window
I felt excited, I got a slushy feeling.

I saw some icicles hanging from the tiles
The snow was glistening under the sun.

There were children playing in the snow
Having snowball fights.

Steven Thompson-Friend (10)
The Bishops' CE & RC Primary School, Chelmsford

The Blanket Of Snow

When I looked at the snow
It was like a huge swimming pool
The kids were whirling round and round.

It smelt like frozen fresh milk
And looked like glistening silk
In the daylight sun.

It felt like a packet of crisps
A crispy, crunchy, bumbly white blanket
It makes me shiver and shudder.

I'm glad it snowed today
It made me a lucky boy
Who plays happily in the daylight sun.

Thomas Went (9)
The Bishops' CE & RC Primary School, Chelmsford

Snowflakes

S nowflakes softly falling to the ground
N o one runs across the glistening field
O ceans of snow are everywhere
W eather permitting snow will fall
F alling snow is soft and powdery
L ovely snow to play in
A blanket of snow is what the fields look like
K icking snow is fun
E very new day is delightful
S o everyone go and play in the snow!

Lucinda Andrews (9)
The Bishops' CE & RC Primary School, Chelmsford

Winter Wonderland

Cold snowflakes falling
On the pointy treetops and chilly carol singers
The snow falls in the air
The breeze is blowing.

The freezing ponds have got ice skaters on
Gliding swiftly on the ice
Skaters slip, break a leg or glide so fast on the weak ice
Crack, crack, 'Watch out, get off the ice.'

The sun melts the snow to water
Grunts and groans from the children
Some of the snow glistens and shines
It's not as good as the old snow
Because it's not crunchy so children are very sad.

Stuart Belbin (10)
The Bishops' CE & RC Primary School, Chelmsford

Winter Wonderland

Snow is a big white blanket,
Covering the field.

The snow sealed the gate below,
Just as the freezing wind began to blow.

When I'm running all around,
The snow touches the ground.

When I'm standing on the snow,
My feet start to go.

I thought of a snowball fight,
As the snow went very bright.

Katie Brown (9)
The Bishops' CE & RC Primary School, Chelmsford

Winter Wonderland

As I jumped out of my bed
With naughty ted on my head
I ran downstairs to my mum
And ate my hot cross bun

I jumped out the open door
Brushing and combing my hair
The snow is as big as a whale
Prancing and dancing around

Here comes a teacher, I'm ready to aim
If I throw it I won't get the blame
Here comes an old man, plump and round
If I throw a snowball at him, it will make a strange sound

I've had some fun, I need my dinner
But I'm the overall champion winner.

Roisin Chapman (9)
The Bishops' CE & RC Primary School, Chelmsford

A Snowy Day

Children playing in the freezing snow
Bumpy areas all around
Loads of snow everywhere
Icy areas nearly everywhere
When the shiny sun goes on
The crunchy snow
It melts it all down
It felt as if I was in a winter wonderland.

Alex Collop (10)
The Bishops' CE & RC Primary School, Chelmsford

Snowing

Snow looks magic
No one will think it's tragic

Now it's down, it won't take flight
Not before our snowball fight

On and on it goes
My toes shiver from the biting cold

Whirling and twirling gently to the ground
Which you cannot pound

In the garden it looks like it's hardened
Under the white blanket

Gee, my lizard doesn't look happy
Unlike the other children.

Adam Cresswell (10)
The Bishops' CE & RC Primary School, Chelmsford

Snow

It's a lovely day,
We can go out and play.

Be careful of the slippery snow,
People walking slow.

Let's build a snowman,
As good as we can.

There's a big hill, let's get our sleigh,
Whee, this is a lovely day.

Oh now it's all melting,
It's a lovely day but we can't play.

Lianne Shepherd (9)
The Bishops' CE & RC Primary School, Chelmsford

Snow In The Playground

Snow in the playground, but I don't care,
I'm kicking and jumping, so beware.
I'm going to trample, this blanket of snow,
I've got loads of snowballs, ready to throw.

I'm walking around in this glistening land,
The snow looks like a beach full of sand.
Let's build a snowman with a carrot for a nose,
It's so cold out here, I can't feel my toes!

It's getting late now, and quite dark too,
I'm getting pretty tired and I'm freezing too.
I've had some fun, but I need to go to bed,
And I want to play with my little white ted.

I've had loads of fun in the sparkling snow,
But here comes my sister with a snowball, oh no!

Claire Parker (9)
The Bishops' CE & RC Primary School, Chelmsford

Snow

Snow tipping on the ground
It lays on the ground like a white blanket
The sun makes it sparkle like the stars
As you walk along it crunches and crackles.

When you pick it up it's hard and powdery
Make a snowman with your freezing hands
Trees are like white mushrooms
It's like winter wonderland.

Stephanie Thompson (10)
The Bishops' CE & RC Primary School, Chelmsford

That Day That Everyone Wishes For

The snow sparkles from the sun,
Oh winter, it's really good fun.
I wish it would be winter all year round,
Snow gently drifting to the ground.

Having fights with snowballs,
But make sure no one falls.
On the white blanket of snow,
All run, let's go.

Crystal raindrops falling to the ground,
They are so small, they don't make a sound.
The snow sparkles from the sun,
Watch out there's a snowball, so run!

Heidi Smith (9)
The Bishops' CE & RC Primary School, Chelmsford

On The School Field

The glittering snow melts in the sun,
The ground is icy, the wind has just begun.
We throw snowballs all around,
They fly and then hit the ground.

Everyone is having lots of fun,
Doing things they have never done.
Snow-topped trees blowing in the breeze,
Everyone is getting ready for the big freeze.

We run around in the snow,
Making footprints as we go.
Snowball fights are going on now,
Here comes a snowball, ow!

Laura Edes (10)
The Bishops' CE & RC Primary School, Chelmsford

Snow Ride

Slipping, sliding, riding through the snow,
Looking through my legs at the ice below.
Slipping, sliding, riding on my bum,
The cold makes my hands very numb.
Slipping, sliding, whizzing by,
Glancing at the world as I fly.
Slipping, sliding, the ride is done,
I'm doing that again, that was fun!

Ben Seago (10)
The Bishops' CE & RC Primary School, Chelmsford

Winter

The snow was freezing cold
It shines like gold
People building snowmen
Beautiful to see
All the snow falling in the trees
Now the snow's melting
Now I'm sad again.

Keifer Teahan (9)
The Bishops' CE & RC Primary School, Chelmsford

Winter Snow

Children skidding down the street,
almost falling off their feet.
Powdery snowballs being thrown in the air,
while adults sit in their cosy, warm chairs.
The white, sparkling snow glistens all around,
while the road sweeper picks it from the ground.

Lucy McDonald (9)
The Bishops' CE & RC Primary School, Chelmsford

I Look Through The Curtains

I look through the curtains at the slushy snow,
It looks like a cold white blanket.
I imagine myself as Legolas with my bow,
With all the Lord of the Rings characters.
Ice glistening in the sparkling sun,
Snowball fights look really fun.

An artist walking in the snow,
Shuffling as he walks along.
Making snow angels as he goes,
Painting pictures for Christmas cards.
Carrying his easel with all his might,
Can't wait to get his heater tonight.

Jamie Haines (9)
The Bishops' CE & RC Primary School, Chelmsford

Outside In The Playground

Outside in the playground it's as cold as the South Pole
The snow is as soft as dogs' fur and snow is as hard as stone
The pond is an ice pool and snow is on the fence
The snow melts like ice cream
It looks like a bowl of milk
I jump into the snow
And the sky looks like there's snow in the air
The snow tastes like water
I can't wait until it snows again
On top of the tress snow gathers.

Conor Stephens (10)
The Bishops' CE & RC Primary School, Chelmsford

Snow Is The Best, Better Than All The Rest

Frozen ice,
Look at the snow that melted,
The dew is very nice.

Snow is the best,
Better than all the rest.

The snow is glistening,
Snow is like a white blanket,
Snowfall gleaming.

Snow is the best,
Better than all the rest.

I feel the snow, it's all mushy,
And all very soft,
And all very slushy.

Snow is the best,
Better than all the rest.

Look and see the white snow,
It's only 2 inches,
That's very low.

Snow is the best,
Better than all the rest.

In the garden it's very rough,
But a winter wonderland,
I scrape the snow off my car,
It's very tough.

Snow is the best,
Better than all the rest.

Danielle Bailey (10)
The Bishops' CE & RC Primary School, Chelmsford

I Love Snow

Out of my bedroom window,
I see a world of ice,
Cold and hard as I think of
Snowball fights.

As I shuffle along the road,
I slip and nearly fall,
I imagine myself and friends
Having a great time in the snow.

Building snowman in the snow,
Having snowball fights,
Excited to be in this magic world
As I think of more snow tonight.

Emily Siddaway (9)
The Bishops' CE & RC Primary School, Chelmsford

The Snowy Day

When I peered outside
The ground was a humungous sheet of white
When I first touched it, it made my eyes water
I walked to school crunching as I went
With the ice sparkling in the distance
On the other side of the street
Children played snowball fights
It looked fun
People walked steadily down the street.

George Cove (9)
The Bishops' CE & RC Primary School, Chelmsford

Snowflakes Sweetly Falling

S nowflakes swiftly falling,
N ow a white blanket of snow,
O h, will the snow come high?
W ith all the bugs below.
F ed up farmers have no plough,
L ovely snow is melting in the sun,
A nxious children want to play,
K icking snow is so much fun,
E veryone says the day is done.

Jade Gibson (9)
The Bishops' CE & RC Primary School, Chelmsford

Snowing In Winter

I'm freezing cold white snow
I glisten on your clothes
I'm as a cold as the North Pole
I glisten in the snow.

I'm slippery and slushy when I melt
I'm a cold white blanket
I can be as soft as a feather
And as hard as a diamond.

Caitlin Edwards (9)
The Bishops' CE & RC Primary School, Chelmsford

The Freezing Snow

It's snowing, see it tumbling in the breeze
It's snowing, now it's settling on the trees
To give us all a good time.

I like the time in December
When we remember playing in the snow
It's nice when we play in the freezing snow
Now it's time to go back to our cosy home.

Megan Evans (9)
The Bishops' CE & RC Primary School, Chelmsford

Wintry World

Snow was falling quickly
Down my windowpane.

The snow was lying thickly
On the ground.

The sound of snow
Was hurrying down below
As I was just about to go.

The field was so white
During the night.

When I felt the wintry snow,
It was mushy like the way I know.
I felt so excited to see such a wonderful sight,
I do not like it when the sun shines very bright.

Rachel Myers (9)
The Bishops' CE & RC Primary School, Chelmsford

As I Look Out At My Garden

As I look out at my garden
I see a world of white
Happy and excited am I
When I see the garden bright.

As I put on my wellies
To go outside and play
My mother says to me,
'What a lovely day!'

As I enter the garden
I see a world of white
Like a winter wonderland
As it is touched by the sunlight.

Naomi French (9)
The Bishops' CE & RC Primary School, Chelmsford

The Dolphin

When the sea comes in
It makes a noise like a dolphin fin
Up comes the dolphin from the sea
Maybe he's looking for his tea
As the sun fades away
It's the end of another day
The dolphin makes a splash
He's gone in a flash.

Ryan Thorn (8)
William Read Primary School, Canvey Island

Coca My Cat

My cat is fat and lays on a mat
She likes to sleep and dreams of meat
What will she do when she wakes up?
Drink out of my sister's cup
My cat is fat and thinks she's a rat
She chases her tail
And bites with a miaow!

Elise Radley (8)
William Read Primary School, Canvey Island

Sky

Up in the sky far, far away
It's as black as coal, or so they say
Way, way up high there's lots of stars
They look like headlights of cars
They sparkle and twinkle and light up the sky
Way, way up like a big, fat pie.

Edward Pettitt (8)
William Read Primary School, Canvey Island

Happy Christmas

Christmas is here, children come out,
To play in the snow and laugh and shout.
Mum and Dad go shopping for gifts,
They come home frozen and stiff.
Christmas morning comes and everyone is round the tree,
Opening their presents and shouting with glee!

Jay Lynch (9)
William Read Primary School, Canvey Island

Special Place

As I lay upon the hilltop
And look up to the sky
I see the birds above me
I wish that I could fly
The sun is shining brightly
The weather is very hot
I feel so very lucky upon this special spot.

Lacey Amanda Young (8)
William Read Primary School, Canvey Island

My Cats

My cats are furry
  My cats are lean
    My cats steal my favourite bean
      My cats are asleep
        Now they're ready to pounce
      My cats leap!

Chloe Gower (8)
William Read Primary School, Canvey Island

Jasper

Jasper wakes up
Goes into the kitchen
And opens the fridge
Gets out his food
And drops it on the floor
What a naughty cat!

Jasper goes in his basket
And goes to sleep
After a while Jasper wakes up
He runs upstairs in the bedroom
I go upstairs and see him scratching the walls
Stop that right now!

Jasper runs downstairs
And goes to sleep
Jasper wakes up
He eats the fishes
From the tank
Stop that right now!

Jasper goes to sleep.

Meltem Sahan (9)
William Read Primary School, Canvey Island

My Family

Sister's screaming
  Dad's working
    Mum's helping
      Brother's moaning
        Nan's sewing
          Grandad's reading
            Rabbit's feeding.

Clarice Witt (9)
William Read Primary School, Canvey Island

Nutty, Nutty Nelly

Nutty, nutty Nelly
Watches loads of telly
Eats loads of jelly
Has a big belly

Met a blind man
Made him kiss my nan

Nutty, nutty Nelly
Watches loads of telly
Eats loads of jelly
Has a big belly

Got a mum
With a big *bum!*
Got a dad
Who's rather a lad
I've got a sister
Reminds her of a blister

Nutty, nutty Nelly.

Desma Tucker (9)
William Read Primary School, Canvey Island

I Love Things

My name is Ashleigh
I live by the sea
I like bars of chocolate
For you and me . . .

Big ones, small ones
Just choose your pick
Or you can share
A lollipop to lick.

Ashleigh Dawson (8)
William Read Primary School, Canvey Island

ABC

ABC
Music for me.
DEF
I like fancy dress.
GHI
Trampolining, bouncing high.
JKL
Strawberry ice cream smell.
MNO
I have brother called Joe.
PQR
Dancing like a star.
STU
I love singing too.
VWXY
Colourful rainbow in the sky.
Z
Perfect world for me!

Brooke Pidgeon (9)
William Read Primary School, Canvey Island

Pirate Pete

Pirate Pete has a pair of smelly feet,
And is lazy and fat,
He has a fluffy cat.

Pirate George does nothing like that at all,
He also has a friend called Paul,
Works all day, it is hard to say but he is very small.

Pirate Paul is very cool,
And likes to play pool,
But he is so tall.

Jack Sanders (9)
William Read Primary School, Canvey Island

The Sky

The sky is blue
The sky is white
The sky is so very bright

From the sky falls snow and rain
Will summer come again?

Is that the sun
Shining down on me?
Now I am very happy.

Amber Cole (8)
William Read Primary School, Canvey Island

The Eagle

The regal eagle lives up high,
You can see him fly in the sky.
He's big and brown,
And wears a frown.
He is fluffy and old,
And very bold.
The eagle is a pretty sight,
But to others he is a fright!

Daniela Livornese (8)
William Read Primary School, Canvey Island

Animals On The Farm

I saw the white woolly lambs
Go into the field and play
They kicked their heels up really high
And then the horse said, 'Neigh!'
Next I saw a nice pink pig
Now this pig was very big
Oink, oink, oink was the noise he made
The little chicks were so afraid.

Jack Myles (8)
William Read Primary School, Canvey Island

A Dolphin

A dolphin is grey
A dolphin is blue
A dolphin has big round eyes
As he looks at you

Dolphins look very kind
Dolphins are in my mind
Dolphins give many signs
The way they look at you.

Jessica Denney (8)
William Read Primary School, Canvey Island

A Fat, Lazy Cat

A fat, lazy cat
With a long, fluffy tail
Slept in a hat
With a friendly snail
A big, smelly rat
Just out of jail
Jumped in the hat
And made the cat wail.

Elliott Bracci (9)
William Read Primary School, Canvey Island

Cats

I know a very, very fat cat
That sits on a really comfy mat.
He loves to sleep all the time.
He sits and watches birds all day,
Especially in the month of May.
He is black and white all over,
He loves to roll and play in clover.
I love that cat
That sits on that mat.

Alice Ison (8)
William Read Primary School, Canvey Island

Aliens

Aliens are big,
Aliens are small,
Aliens can be any size at all.

Aliens are fat,
Aliens are thin,
They'll eat everything - even a tin.

Aliens are pretty,
Aliens are ugly,
Aliens are very jumpy.

Aliens smell,
Aliens stink,
Aliens like the colour pink.

Aliens are cool!

Brooke Osborn (8)
William Read Primary School, Canvey Island

Animals

Meet the ape,
Who ate a grape,
See the iguana,
Who had a banana,
Meet the frog,
Who sat on a log,
See the duck,
Who got some luck,
Meet the dove,
Who fell in love,
See the crocodile in the Nile,
Who always would smile.

Caryna Barr (8)
William Read Primary School, Canvey Island

Foods

He ate some green peas
And then he got fleas.
He ate some long chips
And then he did some flips.
She ate strawberry ice cream
And then she had a dream.
She had a magical fish
And then she had a wish.
We ate some small corn
And then we met a fawn.

Zara Preston (8)
William Read Primary School, Canvey Island

Colours

Sun is yellow,
Grass is green.
I see the flowers,
On the beautiful scene.
Some may be purple, some may be blue,
And they look as pretty as you.
All these things for you and me,
Nature has its own way too.

Natasha Kelkar (8)
William Read Primary School, Canvey Island

Tarantula Cinquain

I said,
'What's that thing there?
It's a tarantula
I'm only a little boy, help!
Run now!'

Sam Waters (8)
William Read Primary School, Canvey Island

Food

For my breakfast I like toast,
Rice Krispies I like the most.

At lunchtime I eat soup,
With my spoon I like to scoop.

I like burgers for my tea,
I like French fries, they're yummy.

For dessert I eat ice cream
Before I go to bed I give my teeth a clean.

When I'm in my pyjamas before I go to bed
I like to snuggle up to my teddy bear, Ted.

When I am dreaming I dream of food
When my tummy's rumbling it puts me in the mood.

Night, night, sleep tight,
And don't forget to turn off the light.

Harrison Mockett (8)
William Read Primary School, Canvey Island

Skiing

The snow is thick
Ready for me to start
On go my skis
And off I dart

I'm cutting edges
As I turn each way
This really is
My very best day

My hands are freezing
My nose is so red
I've skied all day
Now I'm ready for bed.

Harley Skidmore (9)
William Read Primary School, Canvey Island

Outer Space Race

There is a race in outer space
On the Milky Way
They fight and scream
They might have a dream
To win the roughest race.

It starts on a hooter
They race on their scooter
To win the roughest race
The line draws near
They try to steer
To win the roughest race.

Adam Sartain (9)
William Read Primary School, Canvey Island

Dogs Haiku

A dog has four legs
Smiley, happy, funny face
Dogs are very cute.

Joe Denham (8)
William Read Primary School, Canvey Island

Captain Jordan

Captain Jordan and crew
Sailed the deep sea so blue
Evil pirate with a hook
Jewels and treasure he took

Until one day he met his match
Another pirate, with an eye patch
He took all of Captain Jordan's money
Sailed away and thought it funny.

Jordan Blackwell (9)
William Read Primary School, Canvey Island

Dennis

They seek him here
They seek him there
They can't find Dennis anywhere
They looked in the park
They looked in the street
They looked everywhere that Dennis meets
Dennis is here
Dennis is there
It seems Dennis is everywhere.

Scott Stone (9)
William Read Primary School, Canvey Island